The Edge of Tomorrow

Also by Alan Vaughan

Patterns of Prophecy
Incredible Coincidence
Dream Telepathy (with Montague Ullman
    and Stanley Krippner)
Psychics (with the editors of *Psychic*)

THE EDGE OF TOMORROW

HOW TO FORESEE & FULFILL YOUR FUTURE

ALAN VAUGHAN

Coward, McCann & Geoghegan
New York

Dedicated to the future and those who will create it—
including my children: Lauren, Thomas, and Jonathan
who will be 23, 21, and 19 when the third millennium
dawns on January 1, 2001.

*Yesterday is only a dream and tomorrow is but a vision.
Yet, each today, well lived, makes every yesterday a
dream of happiness and each tomorrow a vision of
hope.*

—From an ancient Sanskrit proverb

Library of Congress Cataloging in Publication Data

Vaughan, Alan.
    The edge of tomorrow.

    1. Prophecies (Occult sciences)   2.Success. I. Title.
BF1815.V35V35   133.3   81-17264
ISBN 0-698-11090-0   AACR2

Printed in the United States of America

ACKNOWLEDGMENTS

My grateful thanks to the following organizations for their help in study, teaching, learning, and research:

The Parapsychology Foundation, New York (1966–1972); The Central Premonitions Registry, New York (1968–1981); The Parapsychological Association, worldwide (1969–1981); in EUROPE: The Society for Psychical Research, London (1967–1968); The College of Psychic Studies, London (1967–1968); The Parapsychology Institute of the State University of Utrecht, Holland (1968); The Institute for the Border Areas of Psychology, Freiburg, Germany (1968); in NEW YORK: The Dream Laboratory of the Maimonides Medical Center, Brooklyn (now moved to Princeton, N.J.) (1969–1972); The American Society for Psychical Research (1969–1972); The City College of New York (1971); Human Dimensions Institute, Buffalo (1969); in CALIFORNIA: Humanistic Psychology Program, Sonoma State College (1973–1974); Institute for the Study of Consciousness, Berkeley (1974–1975); Psychic Integration Institute (1976–1977); Stanford Research Institute

(1975–1980); The Washington Research Center (1979–1980); The Parapsychology Research Group (1979–1980); UCLA Neuropsychiatric Institute (1971, 1975); The Southern California Society for Psychical Research (1981); and the Mobius Group (1980–1981).

Special thanks to Robert Nelson, director of the Central Premonitions Registry, for thirteen years of support; to Saul-Paul Sirag and Barbara Honegger for expanding my mind; to Gertrude Schmeidler for experimental and theoretical advice (and great understanding); to Stephan Schwartz for helping me find the way; and to my wife, Diane, for making the way work.

CONTENTS

INTRODUCTION

When I began to investigate precognition in 1966, it was a purely scientific endeavor. I wanted to know if it was possible to see into the future. And if so, how?

I believe I have found the answers. But what I did not expect to find was that this very search for the answer to the riddle of humanity and time should reveal a new insight into how we can transform our lives through foreseeing our best potentials and fulfilling them.

For me, the search has been a personal transformation—from a skeptical science editor to the person many people call "the world's most accurate psychic predictor." By trying to find out how the prophetic mind functions, I inadvertently became an expert practitioner of the prophetic arts.

In a 1973 book, *Patterns of Prophecy*, I told the story of my early search for proof that accurate prediction of human events is possible. I developed the theory that each of us has a *blueprint of life*, much like our physical DNA blueprint, which contains the seeds of our future. I concluded that our minds do not travel in time like a time machine, but rather perceive glimpses of blueprints of future events. Our actions and choices—our free will—determine which of these blueprinted futures becomes a reality.

A 1979 book of mine, *Incredible Coincidence*, made the point that we all seem to possess unconscious foreknowledge of our blueprints and that all of us are psychically linked in a complex dovetailing of blueprints which results in meaningful coincidence. I also set forth a theory of how consciousness creates reality, space, time, and matter, by influencing chance events.

The Edge of Tomorrow draws on my breakthrough research into precognition to show how we can foresee and fulfill our futures. My theory is refined so that it can be tested in the laboratory and in life; it is the first verifiable general theory of psychic phenomena.

By the word *psychic* I do not mean the media stereotype of a person who has mysterious powers others do not have. The "media psychic" foresees disasters, issues warnings about earthquakes, has virtual omniscience about celebrities, politics, and football scores. This stereotype must be able to solve murders, find missing persons, and tell people how to solve all their problems. He or she should have a hotline to God, spirit guides, UFO entities, or at least *something* mysterious and baffling—and at the very least, should be able to see auras, ghosts, and invisible entities. Some people fit this media stereotype very well, indeed carry it off with flair. But it is not what I have in mind.

The phenomena the media psychic displays become trivial when compared with what I believe all of us can learn to do: free our minds from skepticism and put our psychic talents to work to fulfill our lives and our future.

In my own experience I have found the most powerful tool of transformation to be dreams. By glimpsing positive futures in my own life, by training what I call my *dream tiger,* I have found that dreams can provide a channel for the inner self to express its highest hopes and hold forth promises that our conscious minds can work to keep.

I recall having a childhood dream that terrified me, yet offered a promise. In the dream, which I had many times between the ages of eight and twelve, I saw myself as a hairy, frightening wolfman. Someone loaded a gun with a silver bullet melted from a cross and shot me through the heart—on Easter Sunday. But the bullet did not kill me because deep inside I was good.

As a boy I thought the dream meant merely that I had been watching too many horror movies. But now I realize that it was a *transformation dream.* In a symbolic way the dream stated that the promise of Easter—death and resurrection—is for us while we are alive. Our lower natures can be transformed through spiritual death and rebirth. When our animal heritage yields to the promptings of the inner self, our higher natures can emerge to direct our extraordinary creative powers. We are all waiting for the rebirth of that "good" inside.

For me, personally, the dream symbolically predicted the events of an Easter Sunday in 1972 when, in a mystical flash of insight, I suddenly realized the power of prophecy to create future reality. It has taken me a long time to put this realization to use. My wolfman nature, seen that day as a cartoon, still puts up a fight. But the cross transformed into a bullet did pierce my animal heart.

In looking back at my prophetic experiences, I recognize a typical pattern. Premonitory dream warnings begin the pattern. Since our psychic inner selves have developed an early-warning system through biological evolution, many people never progress beyond the loudest psychic signals warning of death and disaster. But with training and effort, premonitons can be converted into dream promises.

The second stage is one of questioning, of seeking out teachers, of experimenting and trying to tame the wild talent of prophecy. In my developing years I gave many psychic readings for people, attempting to sense what lay ahead for them. Over the years I have received much feedback from these readings—enough to know that I was sometimes able to read the true blueprints of a person's future. At other times I would fail by giving in to the impulse to tell people what they hoped to hear.

The third stage begins with teaching others how to nurture their psychic talents for use in their own lives. In the process of teaching, of course, one learns even more: how individuals differ in their ways of relating to the psychic world of images and how different approaches work with different people. Yet by trying various approaches to psychic unfoldment, I have found that most people can find a way that works for them.

If this sounds like a painless path to perfection, I have given you the wrong idea. Mistakes, hard lessons, disappointments, unfulfilled promises, and not a few heartbreaks undercut this path as much as any other. But I think we learn more by overcoming difficulties. When we realize that our mistakes belong to us—and can become our best teachers—we can quickly integrate their lessons into our lives without repeating them.

My purpose in writing this book is to provide you with tools to glimpse your future promise, your potentials, abilities, and talents. By holding up a mirror to your inner self, you can glimpse how best to proceed with fulfilling your dreams.

The practical nuts-and-bolts problems of life and society need solutions, which can come only from individuals who are using their heightened powers of future awareness. I include techniques and suggestions for everyday future consciousness as well as foreseeing the larger picture of society. I present not more proof of precognition, but ways to find the answer that works best.

If my techniques are to work for most people, they

should have the broadest testing base possible. For that reason I discuss a number of scientific experiments with a wide variety of human subjects—the so-called average person. The value of these experiments is that they show how things work for *most* people in the long run.

Each chapter concludes with step-by-step exercises for readers who want to go beyond merely knowing *how* to foresee and fulfill their futures, who have the motivation actually to *do* it.

If this book fulfills my own dreams for it, it will help you to realize that precognition is a natural function of human consciousness—not a strange, mysterious, and baffling oddity. If my theory is right, each living being *has* to be capable of seeing into the future and fulfilling that prophecy. The cornerstone of my system lies in belief—not only that precognition is possible but belief *that you can do it.* You may never find that steadfast core of belief until you try to do it and personally experience your talent of foreknowledge.

As you try the various exercises in future consciousness, keep in mind that the worst you can do is be wrong. Don't try to convince your skeptical friends of your powers— they have to convince themselves—but concentrate on predicting events that have meaning for you. You have only one hypothesis to test: Can you put your prophetic talents to work to foresee and help fulfill *your* best future? If, day by day, as the edge of tomorrow becomes the now of today and the past of yesterday, and you find your nows becoming better than they were, you will know that you have found the way to tame your wild talent of prophecy.

The final chapter envisions a future time—within the next two decades—in which our children learn to use *consciousness technology* to create a better society. It is my prophecy that the third millennium will dawn over a time of unprecedented evolutionary advance in which we master our latent powers of mind to fulfill human dreams.

CHAPTER 1

BELIEVING THE IMPOSSIBLE

To achieve the impossible one must first believe that the impossible is possible. Once we believed it was possible to run a four-minute mile or go to the moon, we were able to do it. According to classical physics, seeing into the future is clearly impossible. Yet there are persistent claims of people actually doing it. If we can show that precognition is a well-proven fact, then we can believe in it—and disbelieve in the adequacy of classical physics.

PUBLISHED PREDICTIONS

The average person's awareness of psychic predictions comes from tabloid newspapers. Would-be believers, however, will be sorely disappointed if they depend on the published predictions of the tabloid psychics for accurate precognition. Evaluating 360 predictions made by ten psychics in the *National Enquirer* for the years 1976–1979, *The Book of Predictions* (1981) found that each of four psychics had one prediction right and six had none right. In total, these psychics were 98.9 percent *wrong*. Even the hits were not impressive: two chose the winning presidential candidate, one predicted a celebrity marriage, and one predicted a celebrity divorce.

If you are thinking that you could probably score higher than that in making predictions, you are not only probably right—but you may be taking an important first step in the art of prediction.

But how on earth could people get reputations as psychics and be so wrong as the ten *Enquirer* psychics? I know four of them and am familiar with the work of two others, and, without naming names, I feel that most of them are genuine psychics when it comes to getting impressions for clients. But when an *Enquirer* reporter calls them up and asks them about a list of celebrities with whom they have no contact, they bomb out just as easily as anyone else.

Not being without sin, I shall cast no stones at the *Enquirer* psychics, however. My own predictions were run by the *National Enquirer* on May 23, 1971. A Cheshire, Connecticut, newsman named Henry Chase analyzed the predictions of five psychics published in the *Enquirer* in 1971 and found mine far more accurate (54.5 percent right) than the runner-up's (30 percent). Chase was surprised that anyone scored above 10 percent. Judge for yourself if my predictions warrant any belief in precognition. My comments are in brackets.

- There will be a strong upsurge in the national economy within the next few weeks. [Logical prediction, which can be discounted.]
- FBI director J. Edgar Hoover will resign by the end of the summer (1971). [Wrong. He died in 1972.]
- U.S. involvement in Vietnam and the military draft will end by the middle of next year (1972). [Both predictions right.]

- President Nixon will be reelected. [Right.]
- Senator Edward M. Kennedy will become president in 1976. [Wrong.]
- A financial scandal connected with Wall Street and with people close to Nixon will occur during his second term. [Partially right: Agnew's resignation because of financial scandal and the Watergate scandal.]
- Mrs. Jacqueline Kennedy Onassis will become a widow again, probably by the end of 1973. [Wrong, it was 1975.]
- The United States and Russia will join forces to explore the outer planets. [Wrong so far. But note that Russia and the U.S. cooperated in the Skylab space program.]
- Reverend Philip Berrigan, Roman Catholic priest accused of an alleged plot against the government, will be exonerated. [Right.]
- Mount Pelée, a long-dormant volcano on the Caribbean island of Martinique, will erupt by 1972. [Wrong.]
- Severe flooding will hit northern New Jersey and parts of New York City within two years. [Right. In June 1972, hurricane Agnes dumped 28 trillion gallons of water on eastern states, including New Jersey and New York, causing the most costly disaster in American history.]

My reckoning agrees with that of Henry Chase's: 54.5 percent right.

The *Enquirer* published some predictions of mine for 1981 on November 4, 1980. As of this writing, three major predictions can be evaluated:

- The hostages in Iran will be tried and some will be condemned to death—but the U.S. Marines will rescue them in an operation that results in few casualties. Shortly before the rescue Khomeini will be ousted from power and years of internal strife will follow. [Wrong.]

- Inflation and food prices will drop, and by next spring (1981), things will be much improved for the American family. The auto industry will make a strong recovery early next year, and home mortgage rates will drop back to 10 percent. [According to the *Los Angeles Times* of February 26, 1981: "The nation's inflation rate fell below double-digit (9.1%) levels in January for the first time since last summer as declining food costs held the increase in consumer prices to 0.7%." The *Los Angeles Times* headline of March 5, 1981 was: "Sales of American Autos Surge: Rebate Programs Trigger Best Period in Two Years." Home mortgage rates have dropped, but not yet to 10 percent.]
- Severe winter weather will plague Americans, but this time there will not be any shortages of heating oil. [January 1981 was about 12 percent colder than the year before. Demand for oil rose in January for the first time in almost two years, but there was no shortage.]

Two out of the three predictions were substantially fulfilled, according to my reckoning.

My score is not always so good. My predictions published in *The People's Almanac* (1975) for the period 1975–1980 were all wrong. But so were the predictions of fifteen other psychics and twenty-one experts predicting for the same period. It should be noted that those predictions were pieced together from secondary sources. If one seeks solid objective ground for belief in precognition, it will be necessary to go to the scientific experimental literature in which odds against chance are preset. It is too bad that fulfilled predictions of major life events offer no proof of precognition—since the odds against chance are not known and one cannot rule out logic or coincidence—while the scientific tests that do offer proof must be predictions of absolutely trivial events, such as the turn of a card, on which odds can be computed.

PERSONAL PREDICTIONS

Belief in precognition seldom comes from studying scientific literature. It comes from personal experience or the experiences of people known to you. Such belief rarely comes to the skeptic. But there are exceptions—I am one. When I began research into precognition in 1966 I was a skeptical science editor of college texts. Yet I was troubled by what seemed to be psychic experiences. Obtaining a grant from the Parapsychology Foundation, I journeyed to Europe for a two-year research project, which I described in my book *Patterns of Prophecy*.

Belief forced itself on me as I became the target for about a hundred psychic readings—by psychics, mediums, fortune-tellers, card readers, crystal gazers, astrologers, a veritable zoo of soothsayers. Their psychic abilities varied enormously. Much of what they said was too vague to be a hit, but occasionally a few of them would zero in with considerable detail about some event in my life. Most impressive to me were those predictions that came as a surprise to me but actually happened years later.

As an example of what I consider a reasonably good psychic reading, consider a session with a British psychic in London on August 25, 1967. Looking like a portly Irish squire, he is famous for his ghost hunts and has written several books. It is something of a shock when he reveals his crystal ball, asks you to rub oil on your hands and transfer it to the crystal, then tells you to shut up while he gazes into the crystal and tells your fortune. He repeats this with special cards. He would not permit a tape recording so I took these notes of his predictions:

1. September and October will be the most important months in my life. [Not that I noticed.]
2. I will get a lot of help from an older man who has trouble with his spine and talks loudly. Initials are C.F.G. [Not so far.]
3. I shall be commissioned to travel and I shall travel quite a lot. [A good hit.]
4. It looks like books around me. [This is my fifth book.]
5. I ought to write on the occult or ESP. [I have, beginning in 1969.]
6. My writing could be serialized. [Several magazines and newspapers reprinted segments of my last book.]
7. I am going to change homes and states as well. [I have, from New York to California.]
8. I am going to live in a house that overlooks a narrow expanse of water. [A good hit: In 1980 I moved into a house on the bank of the Los Angeles River, a narrow river if there ever was one.]
9. I am going to write something that could be made into a film. [Not so far. If another psychic's prediction about the same thing is correct, I have several years to wait.]
10. A legal contract is not far away. [My first book contract was five years away.]
11. Real estate profits come in later. [It must be *very* much later.]
12. I shall talk with Eastern people, Japanese and Chinese. [I did, a great deal, years later when living in San Francisco.]

13. Europe will be important to me. [Vague but true.]
14. A magazine will send me somewhere on the other side of the Atlantic (i.e., the United States). [A good hit, since beginning in 1969 through 1977 I frequently traveled on assignments for *Psychic* magazine.]

About half of those predictions I consider hits. The other half are too vague or not distinctive enough or are wrong so far. The psychic knew nothing about me, nor did he even look at me after he told me to keep quiet, so he was not picking up sensory information from me. But even if he had, he was telling me about things in the future that I did not know about. The British psychics were making a believer out of me.

FORTUNE-TELLERS

At the bottom of the credibility scale are the fortune-tellers who inhabit fairs and carnivals. Their predictions are mostly memorized cold readings (readings that apply to everyone), with little hint of the psychic. I once did an experiment with a fortune-teller, an English society woman who read cards for about twenty-five people at a charity affair. The fortune-teller agreed to my proposal to interview all her clients after their readings and record her predictions. About halfway through the experiment it dawned on me that she was not only making extremely vague predictions that would apply to nearly everyone ("You will cross water soon." "You will be attending a wedding soon") but she was giving half the people the *same* predictions.

To be fair, I should report another experiment done by a New Jersey researcher, Emily P. Cary. Visiting fifteen fortune-tellers—the five-dollar variety—in New Jersey and

New York, Cary found no evidence of ESP. But her last-chance visit to Miss Polly, in Summit, New Jersey, yielded not only a casting director's dream—"the original ancient crony of Romany"—but also some quite accurate psychic impressions about herself, her husband, and her two boys. She resisted the temptation to pay twenty-five dollars for predictions about her *next* life, but at least she found one fortune-teller who actually was psychic. Odds of 16 to 1 make a visit to a fortune-teller unlikely to produce psychic results. Worse, fortune-tellers tend to be con artists looking for susceptible clients out of whom they milk hundreds of dollars with extravagant promises of bringing luck, fame, fortune, removing curses, or returning lost lovers. Beware if you see a handbill or a street sign for Sister So-and-So.

My single experience with an American fortune-teller ended before I ever got the reading. Paying a visit to a gypsy tea room I was dismayed to find that I had to take a number and wait for the reader assigned me. I took a seat in an empty booth near the reader so I could observe how she worked. She sharply asked me to go away until my number came up. So I joined two ladies in another booth to ask them about their experiences with fortune-tellers. They had been there before and spoke highly of the fortune-teller to whom I had been assigned. They were also waiting for her. Our conversation lulled as we waited and waited. Finally, to pass away the time, I suggested to the older woman that *I* tell her fortune. I described her husband, her recent divorce, and something about her children.

"Oh, you're much better than the fortune-teller," she exclaimed.

And so I smiled, thanked her for her company, and left without seeing the fortune-teller. Why should I, who then (ten years ago) considered myself a rank amateur, consult someone who was still in psychic kindergarten?

SEEING IS BELIEVING

My transition from skeptic to believer to amateur and now professional psychic came in steps, based on what I observed other psychics do and what experimenters asked me to try in their laboratories. Like all arts, the psychic arts are based on belief by experience: Seeing is believing, hearing is believing, psychic sensing is believing. The type of psychic work I do now requires a precision I did not believe possible ten years ago. Yet because I have seen others do it, I have tried it and found it *is* possible.

A technique used by a number of researchers to induce belief in ESP in their subjects is simply to demonstrate previous successes by others. If the subject is willing to believe that he or she might be able to do it, half the battle is won.

In my classes and seminars I demonstrate ESP before asking the students to attempt it. For instance, at a recent seminar I pointed to a young man named Fred and said, "Now, if I were giving a psychic reading, I might say, 'Fred lives on a farm with thirty cows and one goat.' And then Fred would say, 'That's not bad. I live on a farm with thirty cows but we have no goat.' " At that point an excited Fred exclaimed, "But I *do* live on a farm, and we *do* have thirty cows, and we *don't* have a goat."

"See what I mean?" I said. And the belief generated among my students seemed a factor in their subsequent success at doing readings. Sometimes just an open mind and a desire for psychic experience is enough to trigger it.

In the U.S. population as a whole, a poll shows 54 percent believe in ESP. As our education level rises, the percentage of belief in ESP also rises. According to a poll of academics, the most believing are those who teach liberal arts, the most skeptical are the psychologists; although the belief level among psychologists has risen considerably since the 1940s, they are still the most skeptical about the possibility of psychic phenomena. One reason for this might be that their research might be explained as resulting from ESP, and not from their theories. I can't say I blame them for their panic and their often cold rejection of psychic research. If you had built your life's reputation on, say, psychological testing and discovered that these tests could be significantly influenced by someone sitting in the next room concentrating on the answers, wouldn't you panic?

When I met two psychologists whose research showed exactly those results, I asked them when their work would be published. Growing red in the face, one psychologist said, "When the experiment is replicated." It seemed such a daring departure from classical psychology that the researchers feared for their reputations lest someone else confirm their results. That was finally done, and their research was published a few years later.

When polls have asked people about belief in the various types of extrasensory perception, answers show a consistent preference for belief in telepathy over precognition. Seeing into the future seems to most people to be more impossible than reading others' thoughts.

DÉJÀ VU

In a poll of actual psychic experience, however, well over 80 percent of respondents claimed that they had experienced the phenomenon of *déjà vu* (French for "already seen," seeming to experience something for a second time). I agree with a number of parapsychologists who feel that *déjà vu* represents the reactivated memory of a forgotten precognitive dream to achieve that puzzling experience of having done something before. *Déjà vu* is the most common kind of psychic experience.

Some psychologists offer alternate theories for *déjà vu*. A theory proposed a century ago—before psychic phenomena were being studied—suggested that sensory input is processed by one half of the brain before the other, achieving an illusion of remembering twice. This theory has proponents today, but they have no excuse for ignoring the cases in which the person experiencing *déjà vu* is able to predict the conclusion of the event.

Although no one has been able to trigger *déjà vu* at will in the laboratory, it is such a universal experience that psychologists do not deny its existence—they only explain it away as illusory. If you, like the majority of people, have experienced *déjà vu*, you have a personal reason for believing in the possibility of precognition.

Think about your own *déjà vu* experiences. Was there anything uncanny about them? Did they leave you with a strange feeling? Were you able to predict what someone was going to say or do next? Did you have the feeling that you had dreamed about the events before? You be the judge of whether your brain was playing tricks or whether something *very strange* happened. You may find a foundation for believing in the impossible.

My father was highly skeptical of psychic phenomena until my researches into it finally convinced him that it was possible. He then told me an interesting story of *déjà vu* that happened when he was a teenager. Standing at a railway crossing on a narrow street, he suddenly was overwhelmed by the feeling that it had happened before. As he noted the serial number of the freight car going by, he inexplicably "knew" what the serial number of the next car would be. As the next car rolled into view—with the correct serial number, not connected with that of the earlier car—a shudder of recognition passed through him. During the many years he maintained a skeptical view of psychic phenomena, the memory of this precognitive *déjà vu* was suppressed.

ALAN VAUGHAN

UNCONSCIOUS ESP

For me, belief in psychic phenomena began at age thirty. Yet, in reviewing my early life for hints of ESP experience, I, too, found that I had suppressed some memories. While in college I had read a book by J.B. Rhine on ESP card guessing but was skeptical of the claimed results. Perhaps, as some critics charged, Rhine was playing around with statistics? To put the matter to the test, I attempted to guess the number of forty ordinary playing cards, four suits of ace through ten. I held each card face down for a moment, made my guess and recorded it, then put the card face down in a pile without feedback. When I compared my guesses with the cards, I was utterly shocked. There were twelve hits, including seven in a row—against highly significant odds (four right would be expected by chance). A shiver passed through me. I was spooked.

The next day I repeated the experiment—with no hits—and quickly buried this upsetting experience in my subconscious for many years. If you have a firm disbelief in the impossible, experiencing the impossible can be painful indeed.

When unconscious ESP manifests itself in life, we call it "luck" or "coincidence" and dismiss it. I recall a multiple-choice test I had to take in the army. A passing grade meant an additional fifty dollars a month in pay, so the outcome was more than academic. I was worried because I was the only person taking the test in a highly technical subject who had not taken the course in the subject; nor did I have any experience at it. Of the thirty-five people who took the test that day, I was the first to finish. My speed came not from proficiency but because I couldn't even understand the questions, much less choose the answers in a rational way. So I just swiftly checked off answers at random. When the scores came in I was pleasantly shocked to find that next to the instructor of the course I had the highest grade. What luck! Or was I using ESP in an unconscious way? It paid off with that extra fifty dollars a month.

SHEEP AND GOATS

One of the most durable experimental findings of parapsychology shows that those who believe in psychic phenomena (called "sheep") score above chance in ESP tests; those who disbelieve ("goats") score below chance. First discovered in the 1940s by New York City College researcher Gertrude Schmeidler, this sheep-goat dichotomy has stood up over the years in tests at many laboratories by many researchers. Happily, though, it is becoming more and more difficult to find proper goats to undertake experiments.

Deviations from chance expectation constitute the measure of ESP forced-choice tests. For instance, if you guess heads or tails when someone flips a coin ten times, and you guessed five right, that is chance level. If you guessed all ten right, odds against chance are 1,024 to 1, meaning that you would have to repeat your experiment 1,024 times before you would get all ten right just by chance, and that you are probably psychic. If you guessed all ten wrong, you are also probably psychic—since the odds are still 1,024 to 1—but you are using your ESP to avoid the target. The deviations from chance expectation are the same.

If the same trend holds over a great number of trials, we become more certain that ESP is operating, either positively or negatively. Skeptics or goats tend to demonstrate negative ESP, apparently thinking that their low scores disprove ESP.

In an encounter with a Nobel Prize–winning physicist, I was astonished when he said that the concept of negative

ESP was nonsense. The guesses are just plain wrong, he said. You might call the physicist a superskeptic, since his emotional response to ESP is so negative that he abandons the logic of science. He will talk blithely about antimatter, but anti-ESP seems nonsense to him because it would wreck his theories about physics. We do not easily yield up beliefs in fondly held theories, especially if they are our bread and butter.

In an experiment in Iceland it was found that people who do *not* read books about psychic phenomena display an impressive ability to score below chance in precognition tests. Those who do read books about ESP (such as you) showed a significant tendency to score positively with precognition. This dichotomy proved to be a more accurate indicator of whether a person would score above or below chance than did the traditional sheep-goat division. One can conclude that a possible way to bring a person's precognition scores from below chance to above chance would be to encourage the reading of books like this one.

An eminent physicist who has bitterly attacked parapsychology has a whole box of books on psychic phenomena in his office, but he has never read any of them. If his scientific curiosity should ever overcome his emotional bias against psychic phenomena, and he should one day actually read about the phenomena he so heartily rejects out of hand, he might find himself turning into a good subject for precognition experiments. Then, of course, he will be faced with the ugly dilemma of what to do about all those theories in physics that do not accommodate the facts of parapsychology. He can believe in black holes without any trouble—even though there is no actual evidence for them—but he can't believe that human beings can see into the future without having to admit that the whole theory of modern physics is but a special case, as Newtonian physics proved to be a special case when Einstein's theory of relative space and time displaced it as the ultimate (so far) description of reality.

It will be a painful transition for physicists to encompass a new theory of reality that not only accommodates psychic phenomena but is actually based on them.

If the science Establishment should ever achieve belief in precognition, it might enable them to transcend the present limitations of a constricted reality—a reality that conforms to their beliefs.

FINDING THE MIRACULOUS

Of far greater importance to us than what the science Establishment believes is what we, as individuals, believe. It is quite possible that we have been experiencing the miraculous all along but did not realize it. Our Western education has blinded us to events we cannot explain by nineteenth-century materialism. If you review your life experiences for magical moments that shaped your life but did not spring from the logic of materialist science, you may find many candidates for helping you believe in the miraculous.

If you act on the advice of the White Queen to Alice to believe in at least six impossible things before breakfast, you will be getting closer to your goal: achieving an attitude that enables you to do the impossible.

If you want to maintain a logical, scientific attitude about beliefs, it is best to play the game of What If?

- *What if* you possessed the ability to see into the future? What would you want to know?
- *What if* you could sense other people's feelings and thoughts? Whose feelings and thoughts would you want to share?

- *What if* other people could sense your innermost feelings? Would you have anything to fear? With whom would you be willing to share that intimacy?
- *What if* you unconsciously exerted a psychic effect on other people to make your wishes come true? Would you be willing to take responsibility for your unconscious powers?
- *What if* you were able to fulfill your greatest potentials? What would they be?
- *What if* you were able to foresee how your life could work better? Would you take steps to make it that way?

Take your time with those six impossible things to believe. There will be time for many breakfasts and many more impossible things.

EXERCISES

Examining Your Beliefs

1. If you believe that seeing into the future is possible, on what do you base your belief?

2. If you are skeptical about precognition, what would it take to make you believe it?

3. Have you personally ever experienced precognition? A dream? An intuition or hunch? A gut feeling that turned out right? A psychic impression? If you have had such experience, take a moment to reexperience how you felt when your presentment came true. If it was a satisfying feeling, you are primed for precognition. If it was a scary or terrifying feeling, you will need to work on retraining your attitude toward precognition.

4. Has anyone ever predicted anything for you that later

happened? Recall your feeling when the predicted event came to pass. If you experienced panic or shock, you will need to change your attitude to a positive one. If you felt that your life was on track—being where you were supposed to be at the right time—you will feel comfortable in pursuing further adventures in precognition.

5. Has anyone ever predicted anything for you that did not happen, but you hoped it would, and were disappointed when it did not? Could the person have picked up a fantasy of yours and given it back to you as a prediction? If you are willing to admit that wrong predictions do not make right predictions impossible, you will have a good attitude for further positive experience.

6. Can you recall an experience of *déjà vu*? Was there any accompanying idea that you had dreamed of the experience before it happened? Did your *déjà vu* experience give you any belief in your personal power of precognition? If you are willing to acknowledge that it might be connected with precognition, you will have the right attitude for further exploration.

7. Have you ever experienced a series of fortuitous coincidences or a streak of good luck? How did you explain it? Did it affect your belief in the impossible? Do you take any responsibility for it?

8. Have you ever suffered through a streak of bad luck that seemed out of your control? Do you feel any responsibility for this bad luck? Do you now think that your attitude could have been a factor? If you are willing to consider the possibility that unconsciously you brought on your own bad luck, you are taking an important step toward the realization of your mind's powers.

9. What proof would it take to convince you that you personally have the ability to see into the future? Reconsider this question after you finish this book.

CHAPTER 2

PREMONITIONS

Have you ever awakened one morning with a terrifying dream of a disaster or assassination? What can you do about it? Is your dream a symbolic warning about your own life or does it foretell shocking headline news? Premonitions are the most common kind of spontaneous experience of the future, but emotional reactions to premonitions can be devastating. As a former victim of premonitory dreams, I will offer some guidelines for analyzing your premonition so that you know what you can do about it.

TERROR FROM THE FUTURE

Perhaps the most publicized disaster of the last few years was the crash of an American Airlines DC-10 jet on takeoff from Chicago's O'Hare International Airport on May 25, 1979. Bound for Los Angeles, Flight 191 lost an engine, rolled to the left, and fell to the earth, exploding into fragments. Flight 191 took the lives of 275 people—the largest air death toll in American history.

Newspapers around the country soon carried the strange story of the premonition of that crash by a young Cincinnati, Ohio, man named David Booth. For ten nights in a row Booth had the same dream, ending on May 24.

I look up in the air and there's an American Airlines jet, a great big thing, and the first thing that strikes me—that always struck me—was that it just wasn't making the noise it should for being that close.

Then it starts to bank off to the right. And the left wing goes up in the air and it's going very slow. It wasn't like slow motion. It was just going slow, and then it just turned on its back and went straight down into the ground and exploded.

David Booth woke up crying as he had for the last ten mornings. He had telephoned an official at the Federal Aviation Authority, but the important information needed for acting on his premonition was lacking: *When* was the crash to occur? *Where* would it happen? *Why* would it happen? *Which* aircraft was in danger?

Unlike news stories, dreams seldom provide details of who, where, why, and when of disasters. Yet the correspondence of Booth's dream with the air disaster cannot be explained away as coincidence. The only wrong detail was that the dream aircraft rolled to the right rather than to the left, as it later happened. This type of mirror-image perception is common in psychic impressions.

Why shouldn't someone scheduled to be a passenger on Flight 191 be the person to experience a premonition of the crash? In fact, there is testimony that one of the passengers did have such a premonition, but that he, sadly, did not act on it. The mother of a young man who died in the crash wrote the Central Premonitions Registry: "For the last six weeks of his life, he had a recurring nightmare of an air crash, and always on takeoff."

Of the many thousands of claims of fulfilled premonitions on file with parapsychologists in England, Germany, and the United States, few have been documented or written down before the fulfillment. Typically, the premonitory dream is considered important enough to write down only after it is too late to prevent the disaster and to provide evidence that memory did not play tricks.

In 1966, after a gruesome disaster in Britain in which an artificial mountain of coal slag slid down over 144 people in the Welsh town of Aberfan, a British psychiatrist, Dr. J. C. Barker, investigated a number of claimed premonitions of the disaster and launched a premonitions bureau in collaboration with a science editor at the London *Evening Standard*. Coincidentally, I arrived in England in 1967 to do similar research, so I met with Dr. Barker and science editor Peter Fairley to learn of their plan. They hoped to document premonitions and eventually to set up a disaster early-warning system. If they should receive several premonitions of the same disaster, they might be able to prevent it. I then attempted to foresee disasters psychically and sent them my premonitions, continuing after I moved to Germany for additional study.

While doing a study in precognitive dreaming in Germany, I was shocked to find that one of my dreams appeared to predict an assassination and wrote Peter Fairley. His reply came as a newspaper article on June 7, 1968: "The Man Who Wrote, 'I Fear Kennedy Assassination.' "

The *Evening Standard* Premonitions Bureau—set up to log people's premonitions *in advance* of the events they foretell—received three apparent warnings of Senator Robert Kennedy's assassination.

One came in a fortnight ago. It read:

"I fear the assassination of Robert Kennedy—perhaps

within two months. I am not sure it will be successful. But I think there will be an attempt on his life."

That was an extract from a letter from Alan Vaughan, a young American psychologist now studying at the Institute of Parapsychology in Freiburg, West Germany. It was received at 9 a.m. on May 20.

Mr. Vaughan set out to investigate the mechanism of precognition. But he has found recently that some of his own premonitions have begun to come true.

THE CENTRAL PREMONITIONS REGISTRY

On the morning of May 25 I rose at 5:00 A.M. to record some vividly remembered dreams. In the first dream an American Indian fired a rifle through a grating to murder a person. In the second dream Robert Kennedy became me, walking through a hallway; dirt fell from an overhead grating, which I associated with a kitchen hallway in my boyhood home. I commented in my dream diary: "A single rifle shot from a grating might be connected with the dirt shifting down from the grating in the second dream. It may be precognitive, but in a very distorted form. The dirt coming down seems ominous." I took the American Indian to be symbolic that "the assailant will not be a member of a group commonly thought of as anti-Kennedy."

There were also a number of literal correspondences between the dreams and Kennedy's assassination on June 5, 1968, in a kitchen hallway of the Ambassador Hotel in Los Angeles. In both the dreams of May 25 and the assassination of June 5, it was dark, the killer was hiding, he fired a fatal shot, he was someone people did not suspect, a party was planned, Robert Kennedy was accompanied by many people, Kennedy went into a central hall connecting all the rooms, in the first one of which were a group of young people, and Kennedy was heading for the other room.

On May 28 I wrote to Dr. Stanley Krippner, a parapsychologist and dream researcher then at Maimonides Medical Center in Brooklyn, and asked him to pass on a warning to Kennedy:

"If you can think of any way of drawing his attention to such a threat . . . I would be appreciative. If it happened, I think I should have it on my conscience; if it doesn't then I only need feel a bit foolish."

The assassin's bullet struck before Kennedy could be warned, but a young man named Robert Nelson, who was helping out at the dream lab, read my letter and resolved to set up a Central Premonitions Registry in the United States.

While working on dream telepathy experiments with Dr. Krippner, Nelson noticed that sometimes dream responses were for later targets: The dreamers seemed to be seeing into the future. Fortuitously Nelson had heard a lecture by the visiting J. C. Barker on his project of the British Premonitions Bureau, so Nelson modeled the Central Premonitions Registry (CPR) after the British group.

In June 1968, Nelson, an executive at *The New York Times*, opened a post office box at nearby Times Square Station and began publicizing the CPR. He asked for premonitions and other predictions of events that could be documented, if fulfilled, by newspapers. In this way Nelson hoped that potential psychics could be discovered with a talent for future news. And if he received several independent warnings of the same disaster or assassination, he might be able to act to prevent them by warning the proper authorities.

From 1969 to 1972, while living in New York, I contributed a number of predictions to the CPR in a continuing experiment. After moving to the West Coast, my contributions grew fewer while I was busy with *Psychic* magazine, but in 1979 I renewed my precognition experiments.

In late 1980 I visited Robert Nelson to find out how the

CPR was doing. The box number is still the same (Box 482, Times Square Station, New York, NY 10036), Nelson's office at the *Times* is larger, and he now has a computer to log premonitions. He also has more than ten thousand letters, a few thousand of which arrived soon after his appearance on two national television shows.

After his office at the *Times* is closed, Nelson goes to his closet to retrieve his Apple computer and begins to register premonitions. One night a computer programmer was helping him. I volunteered during the week I was there to search through five hundred letters to find the documented predictions that should be registered.

In my search, I was also looking for aircraft disaster predictions that might dovetail with one I had sent in on July 23, 1980. My premonition was generated when a reporter asked me to pick up any disasters in the future. Replying that I would do it only if the disaster might be prevented, I meditated to pick up images of some possible future disaster. I saw a bomb being planted in the luggage compartment of a flight from Portland, Oregon. I guessed the airline might be Northwest Orient. I felt the danger period would exist from late August to September 16, 1980. Accordingly, I wrote a warning letter to Northwest Orient in Portland as well as to the CPR.

On September 9, United Airlines flight 291 from Portland suffered a near disaster when a pipe bomb in the luggage compartment exploded. Fortunately the explosion happened when the aircraft was on the ground in Sacramento, and injuries to two men were not serious. By chance, the disaster had been averted. The time period of my premonition was right, the danger was right, the city of the flight's origin was right, but the name of the airline and the final destination was wrong.

I wondered if any other premonition could have been compared with mine to give sufficient information to issue a reliable warning. Out of thirty-four air crash predictions that I reviewed from March through June, two matched in some facts. A premonition registered April 17 predicted that a plane would crash—originating in Seattle or Portland—during the week of October 13. Another premonition, registered May 12, predicted a plane crash in Sacramento, but gave no time.

As it turned out, the closest prediction had been made by a Brooklyn woman in February. She predicted a near crash of a United airliner, involving Sacramento, Flight 201, which was to happen April 25. Her guess at the flight number was close (it was actually Flight 291) but her time estimation was five months off. It would have been extremely difficult—if not impossible—to predetermine which predictions to take seriously and which to disregard. A major difficulty is that very few of the CPR predictors have any kind of track record by which to judge.

The final tally of air safety in 1980 showed not a single death, no disasters at all in commercial aviation. The bomb exploding on the Portland-Sacramento flight was the closest thing to disaster.

In its thirteen years of operation, the CPR has not yet prevented a disaster but is coming closer to achieving its goals. Out of about three thousand predictors, the CPR has found five people who have scored several hits each, making up about half of the total fifty hits. Nelson judges a hit when there is sufficient and unusual detail in the premonition that would rule out chance coincidence or logic as alternate explanations. So far I have the largest number of hits in this prediction project.

My fulfilled predictions of headline stories include:

- The Watergate scandals. Predicted November 6, 1968: "Enormous scandals in the Nixon administration will come to light probably in the second half of his administration."
- The 1970 attack on Pope Paul by a madman who

knifed him in Manila. Predicted December 5, 1969: "A madman will attack the Pope in an attempt to kill him . . . next year."

- A three-banner headline in *The New York Times* of June 9, 1969: "Nixon to Reduce Vietnam Force/ Pulling Out 24,000 GI's by August 31/He and Thieu Stress Their Unity." Predicted March 31, 1969: "I tried to see headlines of *The New York Times* for June 13th. There seemed to be three lines in a banner headline: Accord Reached in Paris Talks/American Troops to Be Withdrawn/in Stages from Vietnam."
- The 1970 explosion that aborted the Apollo 13 mission to the moon. Predicted November 12, 1969: "Unless something in the fuel system or electrical system is corrected, there will be an explosion. . . . It may be that this flight will be aborted, for I do not feel these astronauts will reach the moon." An explosion in the oxygen tank of the fuel-cell system blacked out electrical power and aborted the flight. My prediction had been made for Apollo 12 but the striking correspondences with Apollo 13 made it a hit.
- The death of Bob Hope's brother Ivor on June 15, 1969. Predicted June 10, 1969: "I see tragedy coming soon for Bob Hope—perhaps even death."
- A *New York Times* headline of November 26, 1968, datelined Moscow, November 25: "Russians Ready for Manned Shot Around Moon." Predicted November 11, 1968: "Within five weeks the Russians will send a manned spacecraft around the moon. It may be November 25."

Other fulfilled predictions were for less dramatic events, and some still wait for history's evaluation, such as this intimation of the Abscam scandals published a few days before the news broke in February 1980: "There will be business and government scandals even more serious than Watergate."

Still other predictions will be discussed in later chapters.

The runner-up in the CPR prediction project is a New York man who takes the code name of Greywolf. Over the years he has registered five impressive hits, many dealing with air disasters, such as this one:

On May 12, 1969, Greywolf predicted from a dream: "In my dream I saw what appeared to be a Piper-type plane. The rudder was painted blue, and the number was N129N, N429N, or N29N. . . . I saw the craft make a bumpy landing, and the craft nosed over. The door opened, and the pilot sprawled on the ground. It looked like he was hurt."

Several weeks later, on August 31, heavyweight boxing champion Rocky Marciano died in a crash of a Piper-type airplane. The rudder, as shown in a black-and-white photo, was painted a light color. The serial number of the plane was N3149X. Though all small plane numbers begin with N, all the numbers but 3 appear in the premonition.

Who are the people who experience premonitions? Two-thirds of the CPR predictors are women; their average education includes one year of college or the equivalent. They come from all walks of life. Although most of them live in the United States, letters arrive from most Western countries. Just about anyone, it seems, can experience a premonition. Scientists, lawyers, tradespeople, housewives, students, religious cranks, professional psychics, psychiatric patients, and many, many ordinary people who are troubled by premonitory dreams write to the CPR. Often they are writing for help—help in dealing with unwanted premonitions.

What do the CPR premonitions predict? Nelson has divided them into fifteen categories, but one description would fit them all: bad news. If you are ever trying to get over a bout of unbridled cheerfulness, visit the CPR. Letter after letter taps the gloom and doom of America's collective psyche: President Carter to be assassinated, President Reagan to be assassinated, earthquakes to drop California into the sea, thermonuclear war to break out, cities to be destroyed by fire and flood, economic depression to happen, rioting mobs to kill and destroy, disasters of every description (and a few beyond description) to occur. That perennial favorite, the end of the world, is as popular as ever.

This pessimistic attitude might be considered normal for our times, since in various experiments in hypnosis in which subjects are taken to the future, many people do project their fears, concentrating on the bad news, just as the media do.

This proved too true in an experiment I did in November 1980, with twenty-nine members of a church youth group. I took them forward in time, to January 1, 1981, and told them they were watching the television news about events of December 1980. They were to report anything unusual. Six of the young people saw the assassination of President-elect Ronald Reagan. Ten saw some news coming about the American hostages in Iran (which was quite logical), with two predicting war over the situation, two predicting some of the hostages dying, and one seeing them released. Two foresaw earthquakes, and others saw various things such as "a rioting mob in Wichita," "an atomic cloud," and (this seemed to be an obvious fantasy) "a demolition derby for all the money in the world." Only three students received no imagery.

The group expressed alarm that six of their members should foresee the assassination of Ronald Reagan. So I asked them if they were familiar with the twenty-year death cycle of American presidents, which would make the president elected in 1980 the next candidate for the curse. All the students had seen media play-ups of this death cycle. So I assured them that it was probably their logical minds, not their intuitive psychic minds, which were projecting this "bad news."

When President Reagan was shot in an assassination attempt on March 30, 1981, I realized that the students had picked up an actual event of the future. Fortunately, the bullet wound was not fatal. But in this case the "bad news" did indeed become a media event. The big media stories are seldom good news. In my own hypnotic trips to future events as seen on television, I foresaw such things as a nuclear bomb being dropped on Iran by the United States over the hostage situation. Worse was a plague starting in 1992 by typhus-type germs escaping from a germ warfare lab in Cincinnati. But I'm skeptical. I think that we project our worst fears into the future.

Sometimes those worst fears come true.

How often might we cry Wolf! before the wolf actually comes? If the predictor who writes in to the CPR has not before registered a hit, odds are at least 100 to 1 the premonition will not come true. If the predictor has previously registered a hit, the odds go down to 10 to 1. Put another way, someone who has already demonstrated psychic ability has about a 10 percent chance of being sufficiently accurate in his prediction for it to be called a hit.

When I asked Robert Nelson to imagine what the CPR might be like should it ever receive funding, he envisioned a small staff handling telephones, registering premonitions and asking callers for more detail. Entering this information into the computer, they would look for correlations with other premonitions. If two or three detailed premonitions should forecast the same disaster, Nelson would be able to call the proper authorities to alert them to the danger. If the premonitions were very detailed—and Nelson particularly encourages people to get greater detail—he might even be able to tell authorities exactly how to avert some disaster.

In his future vision Nelson would be working with a handful of psychic predictors who had demonstrated their ability by past hits. He could call on them to check out psychically premonitions from others and eventually to reach a consensus on whether a real danger existed or not. With funding, the Central Premonitions Registry could prove to be an excellent investment in disaster prevention. But it would take not only money but hard work, much in the same way the police must check out hundreds of leads before finding the one that cracks the case.

As things stand now, it will probably take an accurate premonition of a space shuttle crash or the next nuclear plant disaster before governmental minds will finally realize that prevention is far cheaper than cleaning up afterward—not to mention the saving of lives. If the CPR someday saves just one life, it will have been worth the effort. In the meanwhile, the CPR is succeeding in its scientific goals and as a home for letters from people who do not know what to do about premonitions.

DREAMS OF DEATH

By far the most common kind of premonition—and the most upsetting—is a dream of death. The annals of psychical research show thousands of claims of fulfilled death premonitions. But if *unfulfilled* death premonitions were collected, the number would be a hundred times greater. How can we distinguish a genuinely psychic death premonition from a symbolic death dream? And why do we have all these death dreams?

I recorded my first death dream in 1966 when I was becoming interested in spiritual and psychic matters. At age twenty-nine I had no background in dream interpretation nor any other kind of psychological understanding. So when I dreamed of my father's death, I feared it might be literally quite soon. In my dream he died ten days after returning from a trip.

Looking back on the dream now, I realize that it fits a common pattern. When a person is going through a spiritual crisis in preparation for a spiritual rebirth—some call it a "passage of life"—he or she tends to dream of the death of a parent, particularly of the same-sex parent. There must be death before there can be rebirth. Jungians refer to this process as individuation, meaning that the youthful ways acquired from our parents are replaced with a truer and more complete adult who becomes his or her own person.

In the dream of my father's death one detail did seem drawn from the future. When he died in 1977, it was exactly ten days after *I* returned from a trip (not him, as in the dream eleven years before).

At one of my seminars a woman told me of her dream of chopping up her mother in little pieces, putting them in a box, and not feeling the slightest bit guilty. As we explored this dream I suggested that symbolically she was getting rid of attitudes imposed on her by her mother and was now beginning to do things the way *she* felt was right, without guilt. She agreed to this interpretation.

Another woman confessed that for several years she had been anxious because of a dream in which she saw the death of her adult son. In questioning her about her son's life at the time of the dream, she admitted that he did go through a major change in life, one for the better. When I suggested that her dream signified her son's spiritual rebirth—that it was not a premonition of his death—she immediately understood the dream's symbolism, and felt chagrined that the dream had worried her for so many years.

If you dream of the death of some celebrity with whom you closely identify, it may only be symbolic of a major transformation coming in your own life. I recall when an Italian friend going through psychotherapy dreamed of Frank Sinatra dying in a car crash in 1966; it was symbolic that he (represented by his hero, Sinatra) was going through spiritual death in preparation for spiritual rebirth.

Dreaming of celebrities can often be interpreted symbolically as focusing on that aspect of yourself represented by the celebrity. If you dream of a celebrity, ask yourself what qualities in you might be represented by that person; if you dream of the celebrity's death, your unconscious may be symbolizing the ending of those qualities in yourself. In the same way, when you dream of the death of a friend or relative, ask yourself if they might symbolically represent qualities within yourself that are dying.

Dreams of the *illness* of celebrities may take on a different meaning. In 1979 when a friend wrote that she had a premonition that President Carter was to become ill, I asked her, "How's your own health?" She admitted it had not been good. When I suggested that she was projecting her own situation on to President Carter, she felt I was probably right. Carter, in fact, did not become ill.

In general, dreams of death are a common symbolic shorthand of the unconscious for changes within yourself, and all possible connections with you *yourself* should be explored before you consider the idea that the dream may be a true prophecy.

When a dream contains a true prophecy of death, it can be shocking. It was shock I felt in 1979 when I heard the news of the assassination of San Francisco's mayor, George Moscone. My wife, Diane, reminded me that nearly two years before she had told me of a dream in which Mayor Moscone was assassinated; it had to do somehow with the color white. Moscone's assassin was a disgruntled member of the San Francisco board of supervisors, and his name was Dan White.

Because the idea of our mayor being assassinated seemed so fantastic, neither Diane nor I took it seriously enough to write it down, much less send it to the Central Premonitions Registry. "It's probably symbolic of something," I said, and cheerfully disregarded the dream. But here is what I should have done, and what you might want to do if you or someone close to you has a death dream. Ask these questions:

1. Have you ever had a true dream premonition before? [Diane had dreamed of Robert Kennedy's assassination shortly before it happened.]
2. Does the person dreamed about symbolize anything in particular? [Diane said not.]
3. Replay the dream in your mind's eye and relive any emotions connected with it. Is there cause for worry? [Diane felt anxious.]
4. Are you a participant or observer in the dream? [Diane was an observer—meaning it could be about someone else's life.]
5. Does the dream make any sense in relation to your own life? [Diane said it did not.]

With those responses, I should have written to the CPR. Even if I had been convinced that Diane's dream was a genuine premonition, I would not have written Mayor Moscone. If he took the warning seriously, he would have been alarmed, but he would not know what to do about it. The dream, following the usual pattern, contained no details that might have prevented his assassination: No time was given; no situation was described; the name of his assassin, at that time a man of good standing, was contained in the dream in such a way that it was meaningful only afterward.

As it turned out that fateful day, even if Moscone had been warned of an assassination attempt by some unknown person, the mayor's security guards would have been unable to do anything, since White, as a member of City Hall, had easy access to the mayor's office and the office of fellow supervisor Harvey Milk, whom he also murdered. Evidence at the trial suggested that White planned the murders only the day before. Diane's dream was therefore not *telepathic* of his plans but *prophetic* of his deeds nearly two years later.

EMOTIONAL REACTIONS

Emotional reactions to premonitions can be devastating. Depression, gloom, anxiety, a feeling of helplessness, and a sense of panic can set in. Sometimes a need to warn somebody of the impending disaster or death becomes compulsive. As a result, I am frequently notified when disaster seems imminent. A recent telephone call from England, for instance, warned me that Los Angeles, where I now live, would experience some awful disaster a few days in the future. I was urged to flee immediately. Yet I felt no such anxiety, so I cheerfully stayed put. On the appointed day the television news reported that over a hundred homes in the outlying canyon areas were burned to the ground. Now, when that news is reported in England, it might give the impression that grave danger exists for all Los Angeles. This overdramatized premonition created a sense of overwhelming fear and anxiety in the English caller and prompted her to make the expensive call.

In December 1980 I received another warning by telephone, this one from a young man in Los Angeles who was certain that the city would be devastated by an earthquake on Christmas Day. He was extremely upset and felt frustrated that no one would listen to him. As I calmed him down, I suggested that his earthquake premonition was personal—that it was meant for him alone. The message was to be elsewhere on Christmas Day. He was already planning a visit to the Midwest for Christmas, so that seemed to take care of it.

When I first began to experience premonitions, I, too, was plagued by these awful emotional reactions. It became worse when several premonitions were actually fulfilled. The assassination of Robert Kennedy caused me the greatest grief I had ever felt in my life. My premonitory dreams and warnings had done nothing to prevent it. In my own mind I was an accomplice of the murderer, just as surely as if he had told me of his assassination plan before carrying it out.

Unable to cope with the prospect of any more such grief, I gave my unconscious mind the strictest order: No more premonitions unless something can be done about it. Night after night, before going to sleep, I drummed this message into my subconscious. It seemed to work. No more dreams of death and disaster haunted me.

A technique used by Dr. Thelma Moss, a psychologist and parapsychologist in Pacific Palisades, is to hypnotize clients suffering from premonitory dreams and give them the suggestion that they will continue to have the dreams but that they will no longer be able to recall them in the morning.

A large part of the negative emotions generated by premonitions comes from the feeling of not being able to do anything about them. When people ask me what to do about their premonitions, I advise them to try to get as much additional detail as possible and send the premonition to the CPR. Passing along the responsibility of action to someone who might be better qualified to judge takes the weight off the shoulders of the premonitory dreamers. If the premonition turns out to be accurate, at least they have the documentation of the CPR to prove to their family and friends that they were not imagining things. And at the most, it is possible that some future premonition might dovetail with others registered with the CPR so that preventive action can be taken.

I would estimate that more than half the readers of this book have either experienced a premonition or that they someday will. In the exercise section, let us consider what to do when a premonition comes.

EXERCISES

What to Do When a Premonition Comes

1. If your premonition comes as a dream, write out as complete a description as you can. Often telling another person will jog your memory with additional details.

2. In your mind's eye, try to reexperience the dream and focus on the accompanying emotions. You may find it helpful to enter into a relaxed, meditative state of consciousness similar to the dream state.

3. Jot down your associations with the main elements of the dream. Assume that the dream images may have some symbolic character, and try to generalize what the symbols might mean to you. This symbolism includes both personal reactions and attitudes as well as more general ideas.

4. Ask yourself if your dream images and symbols might possibly refer to any situation you are currently concerned about. What might have triggered the dream? Has anything similar happened recently in your life?

5. Now consider the dream images in connection with the emotions you experienced. If there is some disaster or death taking place in the images but your emotions indi-

cate an inappropriate response, if in your dream you are not frightened, it most probably means that the dream is entirely symbolic.

6. If the dream emotions are of fear or horror, assume that the dream might be a possible true premonition. Then the question is: Does the premonition apply to the person dreamed about or does it refer most directly to you in a symbolic way? The premonition may be a warning specifically for you. Are you planning to do anything that the premonition might literally or symbolically describe? Does your present situation demand some action advised by the dream? If so, give the dream the benefit of the doubt—especially if the theme is repeated—and act on it.

7. If you are entirely an observer of your dream premonition, assume that it applies to someone else. If you participate in the dream, assume that it might apply to you.

8. If the dream was unusually vivid, provoked strong negative emotions, seemed not to apply to your life at all, was not triggered by recent anxieties, does not seem to be a projection of your own fears, and seems different from your usual dream patterns, assume that it might be a true premonition of an event happening to someone else. In that case, ask yourself for additional details of when, where, who, why, and how. If any answers come to mind, jot them down and send your premonition (preferably typed) to the Central Premonitions Registry, Box 482, Times Square Station, New York, NY 10036. If you see a fulfillment or partial fulfillment of your premonition in a newspaper, send a copy of the item to the CPR.

9. If after persistent analysis and questioning your dream premonition seems vague or not sufficiently convincing to warrant action, put the dream record away for later review. In a few months (or years), you may find that your premonition did have some significance for the future—probably your future.

10. If your premonition was about someone known to

you and you are convinced that they do not represent anything symbolically, *do not* alarm them with your premonition unless you have sufficient detail to specify exactly
what the danger is and what can be done to avoid it. Most
people are not prepared to act on somebody else's vague
dream premonition of a danger in their life. If, on the other
hand, your son is planning a long auto trip, and you have
persistent or unusually vivid dreams of his being killed in
an accident, act on it. It's better to feel a little foolish
about being wrong than to be grief-stricken because you
kept your premonition to yourself.

CHAPTER 3

TRAINING YOUR DREAM TIGERS

When we go to sleep at night and dream, the corridors of our minds are stalked by what I call *dream tigers*, our personal guardians of safety. When a dream tiger scents the approach of danger, he sends us a terrifying dream premonition that wakes us so that we can sound the alarm or flee the approaching menace. Evolved millions of years ago before language, the dream tiger speaks in symbols and pictures. But the fierce, highly intelligent dream tiger can be trained to speak in English.

If you pay no attention to your dream tiger—if you make no effort to remember and understand your dreams—the frustrated dream tiger will savage you with unwanted and terrifying dream premonitions to get your attention. The incredible power of this remarkable beast and how it can be trained was revealed in a dream as I was beginning a study of precognitive dreams:

THE DREAM TIGER
I was in a cave, swimming about in a shallow pool, when a powerful Tarzanlike man appeared with a tiger. I was very

frightened of the tiger, but I tried not to let on. The man was bragging a bit about the prowess of his tiger and how well trained it was. He pointed out a large pool outside the cave but very far down the mountain side. He said he would order his tiger to dive into that distant pool and return. That seemed to be an incredible feat but the tiger did it. When the tiger returned it had to pass over me, which frightened me even more. But I worked up courage and said, "That's very good." I was astonished when the tiger replied, "Thank you."

"My God," I thought, "it can speak English." And I was no longer afraid of the tiger, but admired it the more.

The dream's symbolism suggests that the shallow pool in the cave is the most accessible part of our unconscious, but the Tarzan figure—the strong, primitive aspect of our inner self—can train the dream tiger to dive into a deeper part of the unconscious where the future can be glimpsed. Further, the tiger can render this precognitive information in our own language so that we can understand it and make use of it more easily. Once tamed, the dream tiger deserves our admiration.

According to my theory, our dream tigers stem from mankind's early evolutionary development. When our earliest ancestors lived in the jungles, there was constant danger from predators, especially at night when they were sleeping. But during the dreaming state, about every ninety minutes, each one's dream tiger would scan the environment for danger. When a predator, perhaps a saber-toothed tiger, approached, the dream tiger would sound the alarm by sending a premonitory dream terrifying enough to wake the adult sleeper; babies and small children, who were most vulnerable, would cry out in their sleep and wake their parents. Alarmed by this inner sentry, our ancestor would scamper to safety. Those who paid no attention to their dreams tended to be eaten; we, as survivors, inherit the primitive dream tigers, which terrify us but wish only to protect us.

When a child awakens or cries out in terror of the night, don't say, "It's only a dream. Go back to sleep." Tell your child we all have special monsters—dream tigers—for protection and guidance. Encourage your child to make friends with his or her dream monster, to find out what it wants, and to ask it how the dream monster can help. Children seem unduly fascinated with monsters, and will want them as special friends.

If you have experienced a dream premonition, comfort yourself with the knowledge that you have a powerful but potentially friendly ally within yourself that can be trained to protect and guide you. The first step in making friends with your dream tiger is to learn to interpret its language—symbols. Since the dream tiger has a propensity to scan the future, your task is to convince it that you need positive, guiding information from the future. The more you communicate with your dream tiger, by recording, analyzing, and interpreting dreams, the better it can serve you.

Sometimes premonitions can serve us too, but now we live in houses and have police for protection, so we usually no longer need the nightly vigilance of our dream tigers against the threat of danger. Now we can ask our tigers for dreams of *promise* instead of *premonition*.

Dream tigers, like the tigers of the jungle, can never be completely tamed. Although with proper inducements they can be trained up to a point, they always retain the independent and fierce ways of the primal beast. Bear in mind that dreams cannot be *controlled*, merely *influenced*. Even the best-trained dream tiger will sometimes ignore your request or assert itself in unexpected ways. That's what makes them so fascinating.

REMEMBERING DREAMS

If you have difficulty in remembering dreams, here are some hints for better dream recall:

1. Before you go to sleep at night, give yourself the suggestion that you will wake early in the morning with the memory of a dream and be able to write it.
2. Keep a pad and pen under your pillow or nearby so that when you awaken you can jot down notes. You can substitute a tape recorder if your speaking will not awaken someone else in the bedroom.
3. The last part of the dream is usually the first remembered. Work your way back to the beginning of the dream by asking, "What came before that?"
4. You may wish to set your alarm a half hour earlier so that it will be more likely to waken you during a dream and you will have time to record it before doing anything else.
5. If you "never" remember dreams, ask a friend (or hire someone) to sit at your bedside all night, with a dim light on, so that when your eyes are moving back and forth (rapid eye movements) your friend can wake you and ask for a report of your dream, which the friend can write down. The longest dreams come in the morning, so that is the best time for waking for dream reports.
6. If your persistent efforts do not work, you may be trying too hard. Relax and let your dreams do the work. If all else fails, try the "artificial dreaming" techniques described in Chapter 6, which I invented specifically for people who cannot remember dreams. Some people substitute a rich waking fantasy life for nocturnal dreams, so you may be able to work with daydreams or creative fantasy.
7. When you write out your dreams, give them titles, as if they were stories. It helps to focus on the point of your

dreams and may aid you in associating with the symbols
and the metaphorical situations of your dreams.

EXPERIMENTS IN DREAM PROPHECY

Is there any actual scientific proof that a person can dream
about the future at will? Two remarkable experimental
studies done at the Maimonides Dream Laboratory in
Brooklyn established conclusively that their subject, a
young Englishman named Malcolm Bessent, was able to
train his dream tiger to foresee randomly created events of
the next day more than 60 percent of the time.

In the first Bessent study, the targets about which he
was to dream were multisensory experiences built around a
randomly chosen picture and word. For instance, when the
randomly chosen word was "parka hood," a picture of an
Eskimo wearing a parka hood was chosen, Bessent was led
into a room covered with white sheets to represent the Arc-
tic, he listened to *Finlandia* by Sibelius, and had ice put
down his back.

The night before the targets were chosen, Bessent
dreamed of standing in a room "surrounded by white, talking to a black man with gray-white hair" [like the Eskimo],
and "ice blue and white." Three independent judges, who
did not know which targets went with which dreams,
ranked five out of eight attempts as direct hits (62.5 percent hits, where 12.5 percent is expected by chance), giving
odds against chance of 5,000 to 1. That means that the
experiment would have to be repeated 5,000 times before
Bessent might be expected to dream about the future just
by chance.

The second Bessent study conformed to more usual
parapsychological methods by using randomly selected
thematic slide shows as targets. The slide shows were randomly chosen after Bessent's dreams were recorded, by

someone who did not know what the dreams were. Again, there were five direct hits out of eight attempts.

The Bessent studies proved dream prophecy so conclusively that no more dream studies were ever done to prove precognition. The point had been made.

Many different subjects from all walks of life, both with and without prior psychic experience, tried "one night stands" at psychic dreaming at the Maimonides Dream Laboratory. Out of 148 such attempts, 111, or 75 percent, were successful. This suggests that the ability to dream psychically is widespread. When I polled the staff of the dream lab with a 300-word adjective checklist, four of us agreed on these key descriptors for good psychic dreaming subjects: *adaptable, adventurous, alert, appreciative, curious, enthusiastic, imaginative, individualistic, sensitive, suggestible,* and *having varied interests.* Three of us agreed on: *independent, insightful, original, relaxed, resourceful, spontaneous, uninhibited,* and *warm.*

To describe poor subjects, we agreed on only one word: *apathetic.* Three of us agreed that poor subjects were: *aloof, anxious, argumentative, conservative, conventional, despondent, nervous,* and *tense.* If you think you are better described by the adjectives for the good subjects rather than those for the bad subjects, you will probably have success at training your dream tiger.

DREAM SYMBOLS

During the two years I worked as a dream subject at the Maimonides Dream Laboratory I found myself getting enormous experience at dream interpretation. By comparing my dreams with target pictures used in telepathy experiments, I acquired the knack of seeing how dreams symbolize and distort literal elements. The thing to look for is a basic thematic statement, for which each person might have an individual metaphor. In preparation for writing up the lab's ten years of research material for the book *Dream Telepathy*, I reviewed literally thousands of dreams, looking for symbolic correspondences to pictures and life situations. Because independent judges had already blindly judged correspondences between dreams and targets, it became easy to see what guided their judgment. Contrary to what some physiological dream researchers say, there really *are* meaningful symbols in our dreams and they can be objectively identified. In my estimation, the ten-year body of the Maimonides psychic dream work offers the best scientific evidence that our dream symbols correspond to an external reality.

One way to sharpen your intuitive understanding of symbolic meanings would be to read the book *Dream Telepathy*, which relates hundreds of event-dream symbol correspondences. These correspondences are not derived from anyone's theory but represent the work of many judges objectively trying to match many people's dreams with many target pictures. Contrary to Sigmund Freud's assertion that dream symbols are a deliberate concealment of the dream's real content by the unconscious mind, the dream telepathy work suggests that symbols are a universal language of dreams and are easily translated once the basic principles are grasped. Our dream tigers spring from an era millions of years ago when symbols were the only tools of communication. Symbols still retain their great impact and emotional power.

Although dream symbols show a universal ability to communicate basic themes, their specific meaning for us as individuals can be highly complex and often rich in double meanings: Our individual dream symbols are derived from our personal experiences and attitudes. The context in which they appear can also alter their meaning, as with words, which are also symbols. If you have any dream books that purport to tell you specific meanings for dream symbols, throw them out and start compiling your own personal symbol lexicon. Your dream tiger wants to be appreciated as an individual, with idiosyncratic symbols that can best be appreciated by *you.*

Of my several dream researcher friends, the most experienced at analyzing dream symbols is Patricia Garfield, who has recorded more than 13,000 dreams since she was a teenager. She may hold a world's record for the number of recorded dreams. Author of the popular book *Creative Dreaming,* Dr. Garfield displays an uncanny knack of getting to the heart of a person's dream image by asking just a few questions, such as "Does that remind you of anything going on in your life just now?" or "What are your feelings about that image or symbol?"

Our colleague in a dream group, Dr. Gayle Delaney, proposed a method of questioning that even the most inexperienced dream interpreter could use for starters. She asks, "If I were from a different planet, how would you define that dream image or symbol? Who or what is it? What is your attitude toward it? Assume I never heard of it, and explain everything." She would then elicit a complete description of the dream person or symbol from the dreamer's point of view. It became obvious that the subject's dream tiger was using that symbol as shorthand to represent several things simultaneously, and often at different levels of meaning. (For extensive examples see Gayle Delaney's book *Living Your Dreams.*)

Our dream group would take up to two hours just to analyze one dream thoroughly, with six people working on it. We often found that our varying approaches meshed to produce a multitiered structure of dream meanings. We worked at it until the dreamer said, "Aha! Now I know what it means." That click of recognition of your dream tiger's message comes in a creative uprush of intuitive *knowing.*

Here is a dream of mine our group worked on in February 1978, when I was working on my last book, *Incredible Coincidence*, and having difficulty finding the right tone and point of view:

THE PRISONER

I was being held prisoner with a group of people in a building. We were watched, but I managed to squeeze through a small doorway to freedom—an office where I found an important book. Outside was confusion and riots. I was given a ticket by a policeman for being naked. I complained that I had just gotten free from a kidnapping, and the police went in search of the kidnappers. Yet somehow I wound up again in the prison.

My analysis was: Is this symbolic of my imprisoning my thoughts on the book to conform to peer pressure? Being naked when outside the prison might symbolize freedom of my own thought, baring my soul. I may get some censure (a ticket) but it's better than being back in prison.

When Patricia Garfield's husband, Zal, asked me, "Who are the villains?" I suddenly realized that the villains, or kidnappers, were not my colleagues, but rather the skeptics. It was the skeptics who would censure me and keep me a prisoner of my own timidity, my own attempts to conform to their point of view. I resolved to find that doorway to freedom and my office where I could write that important book. I should not write books for skeptics because they don't read books that disagree with their point of view. I freed myself from that self-imposed prison, and bared my naked feelings about what I really thought. My dream tiger's message got through to me.

CALL THE DREAM TIGER

One evening I asked Dr. Garfield if, in the course of recording and analyzing 13,000 dreams, she had encountered any that seemed precognitive. Only very trivial ones, she said. I told the group of my experiences in future dreaming and emphasized the role played by our conscious will in calling up a precognitive dream. Even just becoming intrigued by the topic tends to call on the dream tiger.

A few weeks later Garfield told me of a major precognitive dream. Although she didn't realize it at the time, the dream not only answered her question about someone but also told her where he would move in the future. The situation was this: Garfield had lost contact with her Chinese meditation teacher, Mr. K, who lived in the North Beach area of San Francisco but was always difficult to find. She felt an urgent need to ask him for help in her meditation techniques, but could not locate him at the regular meeting place. His students didn't know where he was, either. The next time she stopped at the meeting place, it was closed.

Then the Garfields went to Hawaii for a vacation, but she was still wondering how to contact the elusive Mr. K. She had a dream in which Mr. K telephoned to say he was around the corner from where the Garfields lived, near the tennis courts. Could he visit her? Garfield noted that the dream telephone voice seemed "warbly" and very emotional. But she dismissed the dream as wish fulfillment.

When she returned to San Francisco, she attempted once again to make contact with Mr. K. Eventually, she heard that he had moved to her own neighborhood, many miles from North Beach. The first clue came when the Garfield's maid recognized Mr. K at a nearby bus stop. That confirmed he was in the area.

A few days later, driving home from the doctor's office, Garfield acted on an impulse to drive by the bus stop in search of Mr. K. There he was—munching on an apple. Mr. K had moved to the very next block, next to the tennis courts—as in her dream. With her new neighbor Garfield studied intensively the meditation techniques she described in her book *Pathway to Ecstasy: The Dream Mandala.*

Patricia Garfield's dream tiger not only answered her question with psychic information but signaled that an important relationship was about to develop. A clue to the dream's psychic origin was the "warbly" voice on the telephone—since psychic dreams about others often contain images of unusual communication. Once the topic of precognitive dreaming was brought up, Garfield's dream tiger delivered the psychic goods in a straightforward description of where Mr. K would move. It will be interesting to see if more of Garfield's dreams contain psychic information now that her dream tiger has demonstrated its prowess at future consciousness.

At one of my seminars in Chicago, my students called up their dream tigers to search for a lion. Before the final day of the seminar, I gave the group some examples of dream precognition and told them they had a nocturnal homework assignment: Dream about what would happen to them the next morning. I gave them the suggestion that they would have a vivid dream about the future experience and would be able to remember it and write it down. I had no idea what we would be doing the next morning; I had only the plan to build a target experience around whatever symbol should appear in my own dream the next morning. I dreamed of someone riding a lion around a fountain and being chased by others. Locating a book with a picture of a lion, I returned to the seminar room now armed with a plan.

All the students but one had remembered and recorded dreams, which we filed away until later. The young man who had no dream received as punishment the role of the lion. We used chairs to construct a fountainlike circle in the middle of the room, a young woman volunteered to ride our "lion," and the rest of us gave noisy chase around the "fountain." It was a good excuse to act like kids again, and we all enjoyed our rousing chase around the fountain where we paused to look at the picture of the lion. Our two-footed lion was becoming weary from his four-footed flight, so we called an end to our target experience and the students went to retrieve their dreams.

Remarkably, all the students who reported dreams had in fact dreamed about some aspect of the morning's experience, each from their own point of view, interests, and concerns. No one dreamed about a lion, but about the human interaction that took place, provoked by my dream about a lion. The group agreed the experiment was a smashing success; it showed them that they could call upon their dream tiger at will.

GUIDING DREAMS

What we often need from our dreams is guidance about our present situation—help in solving the problem that confronts us right now. Then it's time to call the dream tiger for a guiding dream.

In January 1978 I was lamenting that my efforts at writing *Incredible Coincidence* did not seem to be jelling. My research, which involved collecting stories of coincidence over the years, was completed, but as my agent remarked when I showed him a draft of a couple of chapters, the material seemed to lack organization. I fretted about this for months. Finally, I called on my dream tiger for guidance.

I dreamed that I was looking at Carl Jung's book entitled *Synchronicity* (meaningful coincidence). The chapters were short, with long titles written in script. The chapters were subdivided into cases, which were numbered in Roman numerals. I saw the opening page of a chapter printed as "The Search for Eliot Carter, Case *xxi*," and centered on the page. The whole effect was quite aesthetic. I wondered if it were an idea for *my* book on synchronicity.

I had seen Jung's book *Synchronicity*, a recent trade paperback, but had not bought it since I had his original essay. But the dream prompted me to purchase it and to note that it bore a Roman numeral series number, *xx*, of the Bollingen Series. My book would follow it, symbolically, becoming *xxi*. Until this dream I had not considered using cases, case titles, and case numbers. But when I tried writing the book that way, it began to flow and felt right.

Taking the dream's advice, I actually did title a chapter "The Search for Eliot Carter." Significantly, that chapter deals with writers making use of coincidence and psychic sensing to find the material they need for their books. My dream tiger provided both literal and symbolic guidance, nicely printed out in English.

In January 1981 my problem pattern asserted itself once more: How to do the book at hand? As before, I had been fretting for several months and was becoming increasingly dissatisfied with my outline. The writing was not flowing. I knew this meant that something was wrong in the book's organization and viewpoint. But what? And what to do about it? The deadline for the manuscript's submission had already passed, so I issued an emergency call for the dream tiger. I dictated suggestions into my tape recorder and played them back before I went to sleep:

Recall the last time you conquered a similar situation. How did you feel? (I felt excited, enthusiastic, inspired.) The last time I had a guiding dream. I need a guiding dream now. I need a dream that will inspire me, excite me, make me enthusiastic, and give me the plan. If it is not the right time to do this, I must know that too. I need to hear from my dream

tiger. Expect a dream early in the morning and record it—
no matter what the dream is.

That night I awoke several times with dreams but
strangely, when I arose early in the morning to write them
down, I forgot them. I was about to reproach myself for
this, when suddenly a single thought trumpeted through
my mind: *Build the book around how-to examples.* My
dream tiger was communicating directly in plain English.
There was no need to analyze dream symbols. I knew exactly what to do.

The emotion accompanying this simple sentence was eu-
phoric; it carried the excitement, enthusiasm, and inspiration that I had requested.

Admittedly, I had hoped the dream tiger would pay me a
visit long before this, but I had not formally issued an invi-
tation. Dream tigers are sensitive and do not like to be
taken for granted.

Although we all want to hear that our ideas and aspirations are brilliantly inspired and will lead to certain success, it is better to get a no from our dream tiger than to
find life giving you a no. Recently I conceived what I
thought was a clever and brilliant idea—producing a television show about fake psychic demonstrations, done by
magicians and called the All-American Fake Psychic
Show. I fantasized details of this before going to bed, and
requested a visit from my dream tiger to show me how best
to accomplish this. In the morning I awoke with a dream of
biting on thistles—thorns were penetrating my tongue and
cheeks. That seemed to be my dream tiger's "tongue in
cheek," humorous way of telling me *no.* I dropped the idea
immediately.

Guiding dreams often displace the necessary action onto
someone else in a symbolic way. For instance, a young
woman told me of a dream in which her former boyfriend

was trying to telephone her. She wondered if the dream might be precognitive of his calling her in the future. I suggested that her dream meant that *she* wanted to establish communication with the former boyfriend—after all, it was *her* dream. Either she could wait by the telephone for the next few years, or she could take the dream tiger's advice and telephone the boyfriend herself. Be alert to possible advice for yourself when your dream image shows someone else taking the action.

TRAINING YOUR DREAM TIGER

Training dream tigers is not unlike training real tigers: A tiger trainer approaches the animal with great respect, knowing that it can never be tamed completely but retains its ways of the wild. The trainer establishes communication with the tiger, shows it time and time again what he wants it to do, and always rewards it when the desired feat is performed. So-called affection training relies on rewarding the animal with treats when it does what you want it to. No whips, no threats, no abuse are permitted. The idea is to establish a rapport between the trainer and the tiger so that the highly intelligent animal will perform his magnificent feats out of friendship and respect.

In the thirteen years since my dream tiger first appeared, I have noticed a subtle change in my dreams. Since I began recording and interpreting my dreams, there have been fewer and fewer images of violence, terror, or other negative events. This change was an unsought by-product of my intellectual attempt to generate precognitive dreams.

My two basic questions were: Is it possible to determine beforehand which dreams might be precognitive? And is it possible to actually program dreams to reveal the future?

Since my initial interest was mainly theoretical, I wondered if there were any limits to precognition. Could I dream about an event the next day as easily as about one ten years in the future? To answer those questions, I had to record my dreams and pay close attention to them to determine whether they might be ordinary or precognitive.

Some dreams seemed symbolic, others realistic, and some were mixed. To understand them fully I had to probe into the symbolism of my dreams. I began to make predictions about which dreams might eventually prove precognitive. And when they were fulfilled I rejoiced and entered an eager note in my dream journal. What I did not realize until recently was that this very process—giving positive feedback to my unconscious—was training the dream tiger. I was not only communicating with it, I was rewarding it with my enthusiasm when it did what I wanted it to: dream about the future. Unwittingly, I was giving my dream tiger affection training and being rewarded in turn with more dreams of promise and fewer premonitions.

Unlike others who have experienced the terror of premonitions, I now look forward to my dreams. When my dreams predict the future, they nearly always give me images of promise and instill faith that the future is worth the present struggle.

I suspect that the true therapeutic effect of psychoanalysis and other mind-healing systems that use dream interpretation as their basis derives from helping you communicate with your dreams and dream tigers.

My dreams showed me that it is possible to dream about the future at least 25 percent of the time if one tries to. The average time span between dream and fulfilling correspondence for my precognitive dreams was 680 days (one year, ten months). The most detailed prediction took 3,057 days (nearly nine years) between dream and fulfillment. In the quaint ways that dream tigers show you who's in charge, this extraordinary dream predicted my appearance on a television show about dreams.

One of the oddest dream-event correspondences in my records came from a long, bizarre dream of April 28, 1974, in which I had a vision of "the land of the living dead." At one point, I came to a stage where a man was acting as a judge interviewing a woman. It was as if they had done the scene many times. *Someone accompanied them on a blue piano.*

More than two years later, on September 5, 1976, I visited the Renaissance Faire near San Francisco and, amidst the weird goings-on, I was astonished to see someone playing a blue piano, accompanying a stage performance of the Monteverdi opera *Incoronazione di Poppea*, the story of Nero's wife, the evil empress of Rome. Never before or since have I seen anyone playing a blue piano, much less one accompanying a stage performance. This correspondence was odd enough to make me consider the complete dream again and ponder it.

THE LAND OF THE LIVING DEAD

Two others and I were exploring an ancient underground sewer in Europe when we found some valuable objects from the eighteenth century. But we doubted that the local merchants would realize their worth.

We began excavating and found an ancient stone pavement on which were colored pictures, which together made up a story. Then someone came in with a document from a scholar, a document which independently told of the significance of the story in stone. We saw that there were six graves nearby; the bodies began to come to life. It seemed that the marvelous story in stone had somehow kept them alive.

The scene then cut to a later time. Now there were many caverns hollowed out. I was sent to inspect one. Each of them was crowded with "the living dead" who went through various routines of life, but automatically. They had somehow been resuscitated by the magic stone. In one cavern there were weird sights as in a Fellini movie. Strange animals were kept in pens. Water lapped at the edges of the cavern. I came to a stage where a man was acting as a judge interviewing a woman. She had a list of how many times she had done penance, and when the judge asked her how many times, she replied, "Oh, you know perfectly well," as if they had done the scene many times. Someone accompanied them on a blue piano.

In the next cavern many people were lined up, going forward, like slaves chained to each other, endlessly repeating the same action.

Then, suddenly, I was above ground. Walking along, I found some money on the ground. A young boy said it was his and that he really needed it. So I gave him the money and accompanied him to the store where he bought food. I told him of the land of the living dead.

My associations to the dream included: "I think of the scene in Fellini's *Roma* where a group discover an ancient Roman villa underground; also of the *Satyricon*, in which the boys visit a brothel where each woman had a pen in a cavern. The story in stone reminds me of an ancient mosaic of Alexander the Great."

Symbolically, the land of the living dead might represent the acting out of ancient archetypes or behavior patterns without understanding their origin. The ancient story in stone with magical properties could represent the symbols of the collective unconscious that activate the archetypes. Most people, like the merchants, do not understand the real value of these ancient things. Yet people, like the boy, must live in practical ways that require money for food. They too should know of the land of the living dead.

The dream suggests that sometimes we compulsively act out the same patterns of life, over and over again, like neurotic zombies. We, like the boys in the decadent Rome of the *Satyricon*, are driven by the ancient archetypes to reenact the same life stories without realizing their ancient origin. We get stuck in a very old rut. But by understanding *why* we do these same destructive things again and again, we can break out of that rut and emerge above ground where we can find real nourishment for our inner selves. By knowing of the land of the living dead, we can free ourselves from it. Rather than acting out the ancient archetypes of the collective unconscious, we must find out from our inner selves the guiding images meant specifically for us, in order to achieve any personal fulfillment.

My dream tiger emphasized this message by provocatively previsioning an opera about the decadent ways of ancient Rome, with the absurd touch of a blue piano accompanying.

The most useful feat that our dream tigers can perform for us is to show us glimpses of our blueprint of life locked in the inner self. By discovering these guiding images—blueprints of our secret destiny—we make the first step toward fulfilling them. To learn the language of our dream tigers, we must practice with our own dreams. When some measure of dream mastery is achieved, then we know that our dream tigers are becoming trained and will perform marvelous feats for us.

EXERCISES

Programming Your Dream Tiger

1. Write down an important question in your life right now, or some problem that faces you. For example, you may need to make a major decision or need some information from the future that might affect your decision. You want to know how your decision will affect your future.

2. Write out or dictate on your tape recorder the following instructions for playback or reviewing just before you go to bed:

> I need advice and guidance from my dream tiger. I need a dream that will answer my question: [read your question]. I want my dream tiger to give me the answer in simple terms that I can understand. I will arise early in the morning with the dream answer fresh in my mind. I shall be able to remember it easily and write it down. Its meaning will become clear to me. I shall follow the advice of my dream tiger.

3. In the morning record your dream. If no dreams are recalled, try again for two more nights. If you still have no success, review the section on Remembering Dreams. Write down your associations with the main dream images and symbols. It may help to define—as if for someone else—what the images are.

4. If the dream is complicated, restate it as a basic theme or short story, ignoring for the moment the details.

5. What emotions accompanied the dream? Close your eyes and reexperience the dream and pay close attention to the accompanying emotions.

6. If your question could be answered with a yes or no, determine if the dream story and the emotions are positive or negative as an answer.

7. If your question is more complicated, as in asking for information about the future, consider the basic tone and feelings. Does the presumed future event of the dream seem rewarding? If so, act in such a way as to fulfill that prediction. If your predicted event is negative in tone, make the decision to avoid that future.

8. If your dream does indeed reveal an answer, give you inspiration, or some guiding image from the inner self, keep your promise with the dream tiger. Act on it!

CHAPTER 4

EXPERIMENTS IN TIME

Our major scientific publications do not publish *experiments in time*, seeing into the future. The prestigious journal *Science* and its more popular sister, *Scientific American*, sometimes attack parapsychology, but they do not publish the experimental facts they attack. And so, predictably, the vast majority of scientists have no knowledge of the experimental literature of precognition.

That is worse than a pity. It is a crippling deficiency in scientific understanding of how the universe works—especially that most mysterious part of the universe: the human mind.

"Extraordinary claims demand extraordinary proof," goes the conventional scientific wisdom often quoted by astronomer Carl Sagan. In his best-selling book and television series, *Cosmos*, the universe works quite nicely without precognition. Sagan's cosmos may have conjectural entities like black holes but it does not deal with the hard data of precognition. Pooh-poohing astrological newspaper horoscopes, as Sagan does, cannot come close to achieving scientific scrutiny of the human ability to see into the future. Precognition must be ignored or disposed of by intellectual arrogance if the dominant ways of picturing the universe are to be safely held in the vaults of science. But those vaults are cracking at the seams. The cracks gape wider every time a new experiment in time shows that we can see into the future.

To provide that extraordinary proof of my extraordinary claim of precognition, let us look at a number of experiments whose odds against chance could not be explained away in a million years—or a far greater period of time in our first case.

THE PROOF

My nomination for the most convincing scientific proof of precognition goes to Dr. Richard C. Neville, a professor of electrical engineering at Northern Arizona University in Flagstaff. In 1975, when Neville was teaching at the University of California at Santa Barbara, he presented a paper to the Parapsychological Association convention in which his subject achieved odds against chance for precognition of 1,000,000,000,000,000,000,000,000,000,000, 000,000,000,000,000,000,000 to 1, that is, a septendecillion or 10 to the 54th power! It took Neville more than three years to do the experiment, so that means it would take three septendecillion more years of doing experiments before his results could be attributed to chance. Unfortunately, the universe will run down before then—it's a mere 10–20 billion years old now.

Neville's experiment could not have been simpler. It required no special apparatus, not even a famous psychic, since his subject was a student who remains anonymous.

The experiment is one you have probably tried yourself on a modest level: predicting which one of two elevators will come first.

In preliminary experiments with ESP cards, Neville's subject showed great success at clairvoyance (guessing targets no human knows) but scored only at chance level when he tried precognition. Neville thought better results might come with something that the subject could get more involved in, such as the elevators in the engineering building. From 1971 through 1974, a total of forty-two months, they agreed to conduct elevator-calling experiments. Neville carefully counted the number of times each elevator came first so that he could make sure that their arrivals were indeed random. If both elevators arrived at the same time, the trial was aborted. In total the subject guessed 2,807 times which elevator would come first. He was right 67 percent of the time. We know that sensory cues were ruled out effectively because Neville's subject achieved his highest scoring rate (77 percent) when he made his guesses at home by telephone sixteen hours before the target times.

Over so many trials the limits of chance ran out as Neville showed that only some paranormal process could account for this incredible departure from chance.

My next contender in the precognition odds-against-chance hall of fame is Dr. Helmut Schmidt, a physicist now at Mind Science Foundation in San Antonio, Texas. Schmidt's subjects racked up odds against chance of a billion to one in 60,000 trials of guessing which of four lights would be lit by a random quantum process (decay of radioactive strontium 90). Schmidt screened a hundred subjects before he found his psychic stars: a housewife, a truck driver, and a medium.

Honorary mention goes to the pioneer researcher of precognition, Dr. J. B. Rhine. In research in the 1930s at Duke

University, odds of three million to one were achieved by several subjects who predicted the turn of ESP cards.

To produce scientific proof of a phenomenon, several criteria must be applied. First, a proper scientific experiment must be performed and the results scrutinized by peers for presentation at an official meeting of a scientific society or for publication in a journal. The experiment must be replicated, preferably by another researcher at another laboratory. The experiments must be statistically significant—that is, odds against chance must be at least 20 to 1 (probability or $p < .05$). And, in the case of controversial experiments such as those of parapsychology, fraud must be ruled out. The best way of doing that is not depending on any one experimenter or subject but having many experiments done at many laboratories by many researchers with many subjects.

How many experiments showing proof of precognition have been published? Going through the authoritative series, *Research in Parapsychology* (see note at the beginning of the Sources), published annually as the official proceedings of the convention of the International Parapsychological Association—affiliated with the American Association for the Advancement of Science—I stopped counting after reaching sixty experiments. All the criteria had been demonstrated beyond doubt—certainly beyond any proof offered by conventional psychology for any of its major findings.

When we know that precognition does work, the big scientific question becomes: *How* does precognition work? And how does it affect other sciences?

But it is the human question that most interests us. What can these experiments in time show us about the best way to use our latent precognitive abilities? What are the optimum conditions for seeing into the future? What mental strategies should we take when attempting prevision? What clues can be found to tell us how best to use precognition in our own lives?

THE HUMAN USE OF PRECOGNITION

The first thing we learned from five decades of experiments in precognition is that repetitive guessing at known targets (so-called forced-choice experiments) brings on a decline effect. The more you guess ESP cards, the worse you get. An analogy in life situations would be guessing which color the roulette wheel ball will land on. One fact you can bet on: If you try a long series at roulette, you may win at first but in the long run your success will drop—often below chance—until, perhaps, the last few tries. Casinos know this by practical experience. The only *sure* way to make forced-choice, repetitive gambling situations pay off is to buy a casino.

What about Neville's elevator-predicting subject? Two factors helped him: the elevators were electronically controlled, with millions of chance variables at work, enabling him to influence those variables to make his predictions come true. Also, he averaged only two or three guesses a day, so there was little repetition. Recall that he had no success when he tried to predict the turn of ESP cards, with many repetitive trials. Neville chose elevators as targets because they are a real-life situation that can be touched and felt.

Probably the most potent factor in forced-choice tests that goes against ESP success resides in the use of the *left brain* in guessing. Our dominant left hemisphere of the brain, which is engaged for logical, analytical tasks, predominates when we know what the answers are and are asked to select one. For psychic functioning, the right hemisphere predominates, yet the left hemisphere overrules the right when logic comes into play. So the less you know about the answer, the better you will do in using your ESP.

The information that is likely to be right when you first attempt to see into the future includes shapes, contours, visual images, colors, textures, feelings and emotions. That type of material comes mainly from the right brain. The information that is likely to be wrong includes names, numbers, addresses, dates, and anything you *guess* at. That is analytical information from the left hemisphere, which must be trained to be psychic. For that reason, researchers tell their untrained subjects: "Tell us what you *see*, not what you *think*. Don't make any guesses."

Successful techniques for eliciting psychic information from subjects in their ordinary waking consciousness were developed by physicists Harold Puthoff and Russell Targ at Stanford Research Institute (now SRI International) in Menlo Park, California. In a long series of "remote viewing" experiments, reported initially in an engineering journal, and in 1981 to me, they showed that with over one hundred subjects, two-thirds were able to successfully activate their psychic ability to describe unknown locations at a distance. Since they did only one experiment a day, there was no decline effect. Other laboratories tried their techniques with subjects who had no previous psychic experience, and again found great success in eliciting psychic information in remote viewing experiments. Not everyone who tried these experiments got results, however, for reasons we shall consider in the next section.

The next step for the SRI researchers was to demonstrate procognitive remote viewing. They used the same experimental protocol as before, but the targets were randomly chosen *after* the subject made a description of the unknown location where the outbound experimenter would be. The first subject in precognitive remote viewing was a professional photographer, Hella Hammid, who initially came into the psychic program as a control subject.

But, as she told an audience at my workshop on psi applications at the 1979 Parapsychological Association convention, she was stunned when her first attempts at psychic sensing proved extraordinarily accurate and precise. She now does work as a professional psychic consultant for the Mobius Group in Los Angeles as well as for SRI.

In 1975 Hella Hammid tried four times to see into the future. Independent blind judges gave her four direct hits—a 100 percent accuracy rate. Who knows? Perhaps on your first attempt at precognitive remote viewing you may do as well. Here is what Hammid described before outbound experimenter Harold Puthoff arrived on the four scenes.

1. "Some kind of congealing tar, or maybe an area of condensed lava . . . that has oozed out to fill up some kind of boundaries." [Dr. Puthoff arrived at the Palo Alto Yacht Harbor to find it filled with mud.]
2. "A formal garden, very well manicured." [Puthoff visited the formal garden at Stanford University Hospital.]
3. "A black iron triangle that someone had somehow walked into." She heard a "squeak, squeak, about once a second." [Puthoff went to a child's playground and amused himself on a swing shaped like a triangle. It squeaked.]
4. "A very tall structure located among city streets covered with Tiffanylike glass." [Puthoff visited the Palo Alto City Hall, resplendent with its glass windows.]

This information about the four target locales made the judging very easy; anyone could tell them apart.

In fact, it seemed too easy. When a young researcher

named John Bisaha, at Mundelein College in Chicago, heard about the experiment, he challenged the SRI claim that anyone could do it. A Chicago television station asked Bisaha to arrange an informal precognitive remote viewing experiment in Chicago. To everyone's shock, it worked. It worked so well that it launched Bisaha into a new career: doing precognitive remote perception experiments. His colleague in these experiments was one of his students at the time, Brenda Dunne, who had no previous psychic experience. Dunne is now a member of the Princeton University Research Staff, where she continues to pursue her interest in this field. Bisaha now serves on the advisory board of the Midwest Parapsychological Research Institute in Chicago, headed by Nancy Solomon, another of his former students.

Beware if you set out to challenge psychic claims by doing experiments to disprove them. You may end up as a parapsychologist!

Let's look at a couple of good examples of Dunne and Bisaha's precognitive remote perception work when the outbound experimenter, or agent (Bisaha), went five thousand miles away to Eastern Europe and the percipient (Dunne) was asked to describe 24 hours ahead of time where he would be at a prearranged time for five consecutive days. The outbound experimenter had no planned itinerary, so the percipient had no idea of the nature or locations of the eventual targets.

1. The target locale was a "flying-saucer" restaurant on the Danube River, Bratislava, Czechoslovakia. The building was circular, raised on pillars high into the air above a footbridge near the bank of the river.

The percipient foresaw the agent being "near water . . . a very large expanse of water . . . boats . . . vertical lines like poles . . . a circular shape like a merry-go-round . . . it seems to have height, maybe with poles . . . a dark fence along a walk . . . like a path or walkway . . . a boardwalk and there's a fence along it."

2. The target was the Exhibition of Economic Achievement of the USSR, Moscow. In front there is a huge iron gate within a stone archway, ornate and carved. The agent noted that there was "building after building inside. A Museum of Science and Industry based on a Disneyland format."

The percipient foresaw "a busy, urban sort of site. Busyness, movement. Different shapes and activity. Buildings . . . some sort of gate or fence . . . made of metal of some sort—it's high for a gate . . . dark metal . . . something like a doorway or a row of doorways."

Visual images of shapes, contours, and relationships dominate this right-brained success at precognitive remote viewing. Abstract ideas, such as function (that the circular shape was a restaurant), appear less frequently, since the left, logical half of the brain commands such understanding. As we shall see later, balanced interhemispheric brain functioning—rarely achieved by anyone in our educational system—is best for integrating both analytical and intuitive information. When you first attempt precognition, do not ask *what it is*, but *what it looks like*.

Dunne and Bisaha summarized their research program in 1979:

> To date, we have conducted a total of 40 formal trials in seven experimental series, employing 19 percipients with no claims of psychic abilities, and resulting in 82 transcripts, 80 of which have been evaluated at least once by independent judges. . . . Of a total of 157 transcript judgings of these trials, 84 of these, or 53.5 percent, have been correctly assigned ranks of 1.

That is a scientific way of saying that ordinary people

can expect to achieve some measure of success about 53.5 percent of the time in seeing across space and time. It may mean that you have at least a fifty-fifty chance of success in your own experiments in time.

THE "GOOD" VERSUS THE "BAD" EXPERI-MENTERS

One of the most important findings of parapsychology—with implications for *all* experimental science—is that some personality types make good experimenters while opposite personalities make bad experimenters. Of course, the heart of experimental psychology resides in the subject-experimenter relationship. In parapsychology this relationship goes beyond physical interaction between the subjects and experimenters, and works even when the experimenter does not meet the subjects. There is much evidence that some individuals are innately incapable of carrying out a successful psychic experiment. To their frustration, a number of such individuals are parapsychologists. Although they work very hard, and really would like to prove ESP, they have been denied their wish to witness the miraculous.

Most parapsychologists would agree with me that the prime ingredient for psychic success in experiments is the rapport between experimenter and subject. A comfortable, intimate, and warm relationship makes ESP possible. If you are able to enter into good rapport with others, you should do well at ESP testing. If you have trouble relating to other people, you will have problems. You may even be "psi-inhibitory."

The differences between "psi-conducive" and "psi-inhibitory" experimenters were brilliantly shown by New York City College psychologists Gertrude Schmeidler and Michaeleen Maher in a presentation at the 1980 convention of the Parapsychological Association in Iceland. Obtaining videotapes of ten parapsychologists giving presentations—five "good" and five "bad" experimenters—the researchers showed them to college students and asked them to rate the experimenters on a scale of five for a number of personality traits. (The sound on the tapes was turned down too low to hear, so only visual clues were present.) The good experimenters were rated as being far more flexible, friendly, free, likable, warm, enthusiastic, and playful. The bad experimenters were rated as being more rigid, cold, overconfident, tense, irritable, egoistic, and unfriendly.

Someone suggested that perhaps the good experimenters were a little too free, and might be sloppy in their experiments, so a follow-up study was done with a small group of experimenters who were considered "careful" by their colleagues. The good, careful experimenters were rated as being more enthusiastic, active, flexible, and confident. The bad, careful experimenters were considered more tense, cold, rigid, dull, irritable, egoistic, and overconfident.

Of course, the researchers were measuring what other people think about the experimenters from watching them, which is important, since potential subjects would feel the same way.

When both studies are combined, the key words describing the good experimenters are: *enthusiastic* and *flexible*. The bad experimenters are seen to be *cold, rigid, overconfident,* and *egoistic.*

If in addition to being considered cold, rigid, overconfident, and egoistic, you are also a skeptic, you will have an iron-clad case for the nonexistence of ESP. It will never happen for you.

The implication for the other experimental sciences is, according to my theory, that the same kind of results should hold with nonhuman subjects as well. The good experimenters, enthusiastic and flexible, will get results, whether it be from rats, tissue culture, people, or nuclear particles. The bad experimenters will not be able to replicate those results, and will tend to go into other activities after being disappointed at their lack of success.

HEADLINE PREDICTIONS

Perhaps the most common pseudoexperiment in time is predicting newspaper headlines. This is how stage performers—mentalists—do the headline-prediction illusion: A sealed envelope containing the prediction is sent to some official for safekeeping before the mentalist arrives. After the target newspaper has been published, the envelope is opened by the mentalist, who shows everyone the exact words or nearly exact words of his prediction that matches the headline. The skill of the mentalist comes into play when he is able to switch the paper in the envelope with a paper he has just written out, after looking at the published headline. Magician Milbourne Christopher told me that he knows forty ways of making this switch—some quite dramatic in their theatrical effect.

Beginners can purchase a trick knife that contains a chamber for concealing the headline. When the knife is inserted into the sealed envelope, which is really empty, the "prophetic" headline is thrust into the envelope from the knife's secret chamber. A mentalist star is born.

I see no harm when such illusions are performed with the audience's knowledge that a trick is involved. But when performers misrepresent themselves as genuine psychics, they should be exposed as sleight-of-hand artists. For one thing, the ease with which these phonies perform such remarkable "psychic" feats gives the public the idea that anyone who claims to be psychic ought to be able to do such feats. That makes it rough on those of us who do the real thing; the public has unrealistic expectations.

When you watch a performer who claims that he can predict exact headlines, look for the sealed envelope. The one way you know for sure that it cannot be a trick is if people have *read* the headline before the newspaper is made up and published.

When you see a performer on television, regard his or her feats as entertainment only. Most television producers do not have the background to control proper experiments, nor are they interested in showing their viewing audience something that is not entertaining.

Is it possible to predict newspaper headlines? The one way to find out is to try it. In January 1981 I did an experiment in which I attempted to predict the front page of the *Los Angeles Times*. There is no way to preset odds against chance for such real-life experiments, but I felt that if there were any correspondences with actual news stories that it would be interesting, though certainly not scientific proof of anything. My experiment, on January 10, in which I attempted to predict the front page of January 24, was performed under light hypnosis with the help of West Los Angeles hypnotist Kerry Gaynor. The predictions were sent to the Central Premonitions Registry.

Here is my evaluation of the experiment of January 10:

1. *Prediction:* "A large photograph three columns wide shows a rescue attempt of a man in a high place. He is in pain and cannot get down. A fire ladder is being sent up to him. The fire ladder is shown at an angle on the right side of the photo."

Correspondence: To the *Los Angeles Times* of January 29, five days after my target date. A large photograph, three columns wide, shows "Fire Captain Mike Reagan grimaces

in pain after he and Fireman Burton E. Sander, legs tangled in ladder, fell from the facade of a North Hollywood restaurant while fighting blaze. Eight fire fighters were injured and one died when the roof collapsed. Story on page 3."
Another photo on page 3 shows two fire fighters on the roof and a ladder at an angle on the right side of the photo.

2. *Prediction:* "Drug Dealer Slain. . . ." There are more words in the headline. The story is about drugs and law enforcement. The drug dealer's death arose from an altercation involving the police trying to crack a drug ring. Cocaine is the main substance trafficked. A statement from a police lieutenant (name beginning with R, like Ryan) says police are close to cracking the drug circle because of the man's death. The investigation is going forward.

Correspondence: To the target day, January 24, the *Los Angeles Times* ran on page 28 a story entitled: "Hollywood Cocaine Ring Struck for Second Time by Sheriff's Deputies." No death was involved. There is a statement by a police lieutenant whose name begins with R (Robert) who says the investigation into the ring was continuing and more arrests are expected. The story is about drugs and law enforcement. Cocaine is the main substance trafficked.

3. *Prediction:* A blizzard hitting the East Coast from New York to Maine.

Correspondence: Southern California's largest winter storm made the front page of January 29: "Storm Brings Smiles, Snarls to Southland."

From a parapsychological point of view, the correspondences with predictions 1 and 2 suggest that coincidence cannot easily account for the correct details.

Like any other skill, precognition improves with practice. Here are some tips for beginners who try the experiments in the Exercise section. First, try to sense emotions in the target, say, a picture. Then look in your mind's eye at shapes and contours of objects. My fireman's ladder in prediction 1 started as a pole at an angle on the right side. Only later did the information come that it was a fireman's ladder (function). After you describe the objective shapes, contours, and relationships, ask what it might mean or what the function might be.

The best psychic results come, I believe, to individuals who have trained their right and left hemispheres to work together. In an informal test I took of hemispheric brain functioning, my ability at balanced interhemispheric functioning was highly unusual. After that, my right brain dominated. This has not always been so. In my school days I was strongly left-brain dominated, and have only within the past fourteen years trained myself to work with both halves of the brain in psychic sensing experiments.

If you have an unusual ability at balanced brain functioning, you may have extraordinary success at getting such analytical information as names (or initials), numbers, and functions in your psychic-sensing experiments. If, for instance, you are a writer or editor—someone who uses words a lot—and you aso have an excellent visual sense, if you are an artist, for example, and you recall things equally well in words or pictures, you are a prime candidate for superb psychic functioning.

Such balanced brain functioning will be of greatest advantage to those who have inborn psychic talent of better than average quality. Although everyone, according to my theory, *must* be psychic, some are more gifted than others, as with all human talents. And in developing all human talents, practice counts for a lot. The greater demands for accuracy that you impose on yourself, the greater will be your achievements.

So let us try a very demanding test for precognition—so demanding that no one has ever performed one quite as rigorous before. Perhaps a reader of this book will be the winner; at least you will be able to compare your answers with mine. Here, then, is the psychic prediction contest of the *Book of Predictions*:

1. What title will be number seven on *The New York Times* hardback fiction best-seller list on July 5, 1983?
2. Which horse will finish second to last in the 1983 Kentucky Derby?
3. What will be the banner headline in the *Los Angeles Times* (morning final edition) on July 1, 1983?
4. Which television program will get the lowest Nielsen rating for the week beginning May 8, 1983?
5. Who will finish forty-seventh in the 1983 Boston Marathon?

Mail entries to *Book of Predictions* Psychic Contest, P.O. Box 49699, Los Angeles, CA 90049. To be eligible for the prizes, see the rules listed in the *Book of Predictions*, by David Wallechinsky, Amy Wallace, and Irving Wallace.

Let us practice experiments in time to discover your psychic potential for seeing into the future.

EXERCISES

Precognitive Remote Viewing

1. Think of a friend or acquaintance whose activities are varied but whose schedule you do not know. Pick a target time in the near future (say, 4:30 Friday afternoon) for which you will attempt to describe what your friend's activities will be at that time.

2. Sit quietly for ten minutes and let impressions come to mind of where your friend will be, what he or she will be doing and what the surroundings are like. Make a drawing of what you see, and record your mental imagery and feelings. Do *not* attempt to *guess*; just make a record of what you see. After you have finished recording your imagery and feelings, you may then attempt to interpret their meaning.

3. After the target time has passed, telephone your friend to say you were doing an experiment in time and would like to know what he or she was doing at the target time. Convey your impressions and later show your friend your drawing. Compare notes to discover any unusual correspondences. You may find that your impressions were accurate for a different time from that of your target time.

Front-Page Prediction

1. Your target will be the front page of your local newspaper, one week from today. Tell yourself precisely what you are to do: Visualize the front page of [name of paper] on [specific date]. You will see the featured photograph in your mind's eye. You will also sense a major story of that day.

2. Sit quietly for ten minutes and conjure impressions, both visual and verbal, of what the picture shows. Make a drawing of all the details you see in your mind's eye. Now ask for an interpretation of what the picture might be, such as its basic theme. If any other impressions come, record them. Now ask for the theme of the major story and record those impressions.

3. When the target day arrives, compare the front page of your newspaper with your drawing and impressions. Also check the other stories of that day. Note any correspondences.

4. If there are no correspondences, you may want to check the newspapers for a few days afterward to see if you hit at a later time. If you found an interesting correspondence you may want to repeat this experiment and register your prediction with a friend.

CHAPTER 5

MAKING CONTACT

The most frustrating and paradoxical aspect of psychic functioning is that others may know our own future better than ourselves, that a psychic stranger can make contact with our inner consciousness to reveal possible futures that our logical minds have blocked off from our own self-knowledge.

CONTACT WITH OTHERS

Before psychic contact can be made with others to describe their possible futures, contact of some sort must be made in the present. The most difficult type of contact to establish is with someone who doesn't want information to be known. A case in point is the Atlanta child-killer case. As one of five psychics flown to Atlanta by the *National Enquirer* in March 1981, I tried to establish contact with the killer through his victims. Going to a site where several bodies were found, I sat on a nearby rock and attempted to describe the killer(s) and some details about him (them).

The next day I was given the pants of a victim, and described in some detail the person I thought was the killer (including his last name, address, description, type of car driven, and confederates). A few weeks later a man with that name was arrested for questioning in the case, and the investigation is going forward at this writing.

The other four psychics used varying methods for contact. Two of them spent time with mothers of the victims. Another, an astrologer-psychic, tuned in via birth data and names of the victims. And Beverly Jaegers of St. Louis used much the same technique as I. Both Jaegers and I felt we could have done just as well by sitting home thousands of miles away with some object or clothing from the victims. Better, of course, would have been objects from the killer himself. But links through another person—particularly if they are charged with emotion—can suffice to make psychic contact.

In April 1974, on a visit to England, I found myself playing the role of a psychic stranger to a British television newscaster. He asked me who was going to be the next prime minister of England when the next election would be held. (There had been an election just recently.) Since I do not follow British politics, I had no logical idea. So I tuned into the newscaster—made psychic contact with him—to see the future through his unconscious.

"There will be another election within a year," I said, "maybe around November. I don't see either Wilson or Heath (the current party leaders) as the next prime minister. They will be replaced by a physically large person, someone with a military background."

My prediction surprised me as much as the newscaster, but the imagery in my mind's eye was accompanied by a certain feeling in the solar plexus region that told me I was making a genuine psychic contact. I told the prediction to a writer for the *London Daily Express*, which published it on April 27, 1974. In November an election was held again—it was the first time in fifty years that two elections were held the same year—and the new prime minister was James Callaghan, a former naval officer whose father was a career naval officer. His nickname is "Big Jim."

I know I wasn't telepathically reading the newscaster's mind for his opinions, since after the show he quizzed me with various names of possible candidates but did not mention Callaghan. I must have been tapping into his future consciousness, since a newscaster has a keen interest in political elections.

The pattern repeated seven years later, in April 1981, when a reporter from the *London Daily Express* telephoned me to get my prediction about Prince Charles and his forthcoming marriage. I was about to complain that I had never been introduced to Prince Charles, when I recalled that we had encountered each other in 1967, when I was visiting Cambridge University. So I did make a prediction: He will have three children—two boys and a girl—and will become Prince Regent around 1989–91 with his mother, Queen Elizabeth, retaining final word on his decisions.

Usually when reporters ask for predictions about celebrities, I refuse to make predictions because the reporters have no profound interest themselves in the celebrities and it is just too difficult to try to make contact through reporters. Those psychics who do respond to such questions very seldom make accurate predictions.

The most dependable way of making psychic contact with another person is by being in his or her presence and touching the subject, as palmists do. Second best is by touching an object belonging to the person, or handling a photograph of or a letter written by the person, seeing him or her on television or listening to the person's voice on the telephone. Emotional links through a third person also permit psychic contact. The advantage of psychometry, or object-reading, is that one can make psychic contact with a person thousands of miles away. Most trained psychics are able to do this. Although I formerly preferred to do psychic work in the presence of a client, I have now learned to rely almost exclusively on psychometry to do absent readings, which I tape-record.

For example, a prospective client wrote me in November 1980, with the question, "Can you make some predictions about my future?" The only thing I knew about him was his name and his address in a small town in an eastern state, three thousand miles away. I turned on my tape recorder, touched his signature for contact, and dictated a reading:

"I think you are going to come up with a new idea soon that will be a winner. It may involve poultry or animal husbandry, farm business. This idea may have already come to you but you haven't yet put it into operation. It has to do with sales, distribution, marketing of poultry products or some sort of product from the farm. . . . Get your hands on the capital needed for this new venture. The market will shift to your advantage in the spring [of 1981]."

The man's reply came four weeks later: "A friend and I had discussed a poultry building for producing eggs. The sale of eggs would be by contract with three-year renewal options, with probably a ten-year bank loan for the building. At this time the prime interest rate is 21 percent. This may change by spring in time for putting up the building."

In reply, I told him I felt the money market would shift to his advantage by the spring, and that interest rates would fall. They did.

To get the specific information about poultry and poultry products (eggs), I merely listened to my inner voice. The word *poultry* came in strongly; since it is a word I seldom use, I felt sure it was a hit. If I had heard the words *chickens* or *eggs*, I might have discounted them because they are part of my usual vocabulary.

The reason I tape-record my impressions instead of writing them down directly is that speaking enables me to maintain a flow of imagery without drawing too much on the left brain as I would need to do if I were writing; the psychic impressions might be overpowered by my logical mind.

The biggest advantage of object-reading is that the client does not have to make an expensive three-thousand-mile journey to see me in person. And an advantage for me is that the client cannot distract me, argue with me, explain too much, or otherwise break the flow of impressions. The only disadvantage is that the client must wait until later before asking additional questions.

Psychometry does not always work. There are many complex factors involved, such as the person's own psychic ability, openness, need for the information, and willingness to consider and weigh the information to make his or her own decision. It is least likely to work when you try to prove something to somebody who has no intrinsic interest or belief in it. It is also possible to be short-circuited by someone else, especially in group situations.

In a recent workshop for the Southern California Society for Psychical Research, for example, I attempted to do a reading on a woman's wedding ring. I said some highly specific things, which made no sense to her, such as "You were married in Midland." Later a woman seated nearby said she had been married in Midland, and that the other statements also applied to her.

It is therefore possible to be short-circuited by someone else whose psychic field is stronger than the target person. To lessen the possibility of such short-circuiting—and also to remove the pressure of speaking before a group—I divide my students into pairs and ask them to give readings for each other. Of the thirty persons attending that workshop, every one felt they had been able to experience the psychic. Indeed, there were many dramatic hits by people trying for the first time. Sometimes the information comes in symbolic form; sometimes in highly specific form. It seems to vary with the person read for, as well as with the abilities of the person doing the reading.

How is it possible that we all have a latent talent for sensing information about other people? Where does that information come from? Why does a physical object touched by a person enhance perception of information about him or her? To answer these questions I postulate a field of consciousness (sometimes called a psi-field) that directs the physical body and radiates pure consciousness from the body. Any object touched by it or any person emotionally involved in that consciousness field partakes of it; since the consciousness field is holographic, any part of it reproduces the whole, though in imperfect resolution. When we remove our usual barriers and open up to receive information from this consciousness field—or an object touched by the target person—we are able to describe some of the information contained in the field, which can be about the past, the present, or the future. The consciousness field contains the seeds of future events or of *possible futures*. Decoding the information in those seeds—blueprints of life—constitutes a psychic reading, probably the one thing living beings can do that machines cannot learn. It takes one human being to read another.

In working with hundreds of students over the past twelve years, I have come to a few conclusions about what facilitates beginning attempts at doing psychic readings. First, there must be a *proper context* of people gathered together for just this purpose. They must be motivated and open to the possibility; the fact that they pay money to be there insures their motivation. Second, they must be *able to witness* actual demonstrations. Seeing is believing;

people tend to believe what they see, and open up to the possibility that they, too, can do it. Third, a *group field of consciousness* is built up, enabling individuals to perform better than if they tried it alone. Generally, results get better as the workshop goes on and this group consciousness develops. If a person without experience (such as many parapsychologists) at doing psychic readings attempts to teach others how to do it, the results are generally mediocre. The students sense that the blind are trying to lead the blind, and do not gain any confidence.

At the very first workshop I did in teaching ESP, at the Human Dimensions Institute in Buffalo, New York, in 1969, a student named Carol Liaros told me she was already practiced at psychometry. So, after my attempts, I asked her to do a few readings in front of the group. She was quite accurate in her impressions. Immediately a chorus came up from the others: "How did you *do* it?" When one of their own group did psychometry, it was somehow more astonishing. Since that time Carol Liaros has established herself as a teacher in the psychic field and teaches the blind how to use ESP at her own institute.

In Liaros's regular ESP classes, she often does psychic readings for the students, who are then asked to rate her statements as true or false. Too often, though, Carol would find the students viewing themselves in too complimentary a light. When she asked one woman why she had marked a certain statement false, the woman said, "Oh, that's the way I *used* to be. I'm changing now." It occurred to Liaros that the only objective way of measuring accuracy of psychic readings would be to predict events for the students. She would attempt to answer three questions about objective events scheduled to happen in the next twelve weeks. The answers would be either yes or no, and would be filed with parapsychologist Douglas Dean, a chemist who did pioneering work testing the precognitive abilities of businessmen.

The questions were basically simple, such as "Will our union contract be accepted or rejected on Sunday, October 24?" Liaros answered, "Accepted." The student who asked this question was surprised by this answer, since he was predicting the contract would be rejected, based on the overall evidence in his union, which had been talking about a strike. On the day before the vote, a complete change of attitude came over the union, and the contract was accepted.

In all, ninety-four people asked 285 questions. When the final outcomes of the events became known, Dean found that Liaros was correct in her predictions far more often than the students who made predictions. Paradoxically, the people who were experts about their own lives were unable to predict as accurately as a stranger what the final outcomes would be. Perhaps the students were constrained by their logical minds and found it difficult to use their intuition or ESP because their minds were filled with reason. Liaros, on the other hand, had no facts or logic by which to go, and was forced to use her ESP to get an answer. We know that she wasn't "reading minds," since her predictions were far more accurate than those of the students. The Liaros-Dean experiment indicates that objectivity, even ignorance, about a situation may set the stage for better use of predictive powers.

CONTACT WITH OURSELVES

"If someone else can see into your future, so can you" is my favorite way of putting precognition into perspective. If a psychic can tune in to your inner consciousness to glimpse the seeds of your future, you can do the same thing—if you can become *objective* about your own life.

Not everyone wants to see into the future: Many people fear it and avoid even thinking about it. They fear death, disaster, heartbreak, failure, anything that might cast a doubt on their rosy fantasies of what will be. We are always hoping that things will turn out the way we wish them to. We have strong feelings about our lives, vested interests to protect, an ego to keep well nourished.

Unless we rise above our emotions and ego needs to attain an objectivity about our lives, we will not be able to predict our future with accuracy.

We have a screen that usually prevents us from having direct contact with our future. It is there for a purpose. If we do not know the future we can at least hope for it. It is *hope* that drives us through difficult situations and spurs us to take up challenges we might otherwise not be willing to confront if we knew that failure lay ahead. Yet failure is the best way we have of learning—and the lessons stick with us because it is hard-earned knowledge.

The lessons gained from failure give us strength and resiliency in our pursuit of inner goals. We practice until we get it right. The only *real* failure in life is not to attempt some desired goal out of fear of failure.

When someone tells me that the first novel he or she is writing will be a best-seller, what do I think? I tell that person, write it and find out. More likely it will be the fifth or eighth novel that will be the best-seller (if ever), but the writer needs the practice.

When trying to be objective about your future you must realize that it is better for you *not* to know everything; that your inner self reveals to you only that information about the future that can be useful to you now. Your inner self can give you hope, inspiration, creative ideas, plans and aspirations, goals and guiding images. If you begin to believe in those guiding images, you are more likely to attain them. If you begin to develop a sense of your destiny, you will be more likely to fulfill it.

Spontaneous contact with your inner self can occur in a moment of crisis or in a sudden realization, when all is peaceful. It may occur when you are twelve or twenty-six or forty-two, or at any time when it is needed. Typically, if my own life is a good example, the same thought will emerge several times before it is finally believed by the conscious mind. You have to be convinced that your destiny is attainable.

My interest in becoming a writer first glimmered through at the age of ten, when I worked as an assistant in a bookstore. But I shoved the thought into the back of my mind because that seemed like such an unrealistic goal. Just a childish hope, I reasoned—without substance.

It happened again when I was sixteen, then working in a library, in the order department. I unpacked all the new books and had first choice of those I wanted to read. I read omnivorously, but my interest in science, particularly, was disappointed by the materialistic and unenlightened approach most science writers took. A thought bubbled up in my mind for a moment: I would like to write books about the real substance of science and counteract the dogmatic assertions of blind materialism. But again I repressed the thought. After all, I was only in high school; I didn't really know anything about science, and I had no practice at writing.

When it happened the third time, I took more notice. At the age of twenty-three, when I was studying for a master's degree in library studies at Rutgers, I became quite ill with mononucleosis. As a high fever enveloped me, I decided to walk in the cooling rain. In this feverish state, I experienced a powerful uprush from the inner self that said: "I do not want to be a librarian. I want to bring books into the world instead of conserving them."

I took my inner self's advice, left library school without the master's and, after army service, landed a job as a science book editor. I had no experience, but I managed to score highest out of the hundred applicants who took an editorial test.

The final uprush of this theme before it became reality occurred in 1965, when I was twenty-nine and working on chemistry and physics textbooks. I had a bizarre experience in which my brain seemed to be invaded by an alien entity for twenty-four hours. Since I did not believe in spirits, the experience was acutely painful. Yet suddenly I received a message: *Each of us has a spirit while living.* At that moment I became aware of my own spiritual essence, which began to vibrate though my body, expanding and traveling up to my brain. With this extraordinary feeling of extending beyond my skin came the most incredible feeling of well-being I had ever experienced. My spiritual essence, or consciousness field, pushed the alien entity out of my head and continued to expand, leading me into another dimension beyond time and space. For about two hours afterward I was able to perceive thoughts and feelings from others and sense events in the future. I was in contact with my inner self.

My first thought was, maybe I'm going crazy. But if I'm not—and this must have happened to other people—it's more important than any of the science books that I've been editing. As I delved into the field of parapsychology, I found that extraordinary experiences have indeed happened to many people: I resolved to write about my experiences and learn more about these uncanny talents. I enrolled in a writing course, and took my first steps at fulfilling a destiny I had glimpsed, but disbelieved, as a child. I took up the study of parapsychology as a profession and found myself squarely in the middle of the greatest mysteries of science. I had seen it, so I believed it—and could finally disbelieve those clever skeptics who argued away humankind's most extraordinary powers.

I suspect that most of us have intimations of our destiny at a young age but suppress them because our destinies seem to be beyond our skill or attainment. But, somehow, through the years, we manage to accumulate skills and to glean bits and pieces of our destined understanding. With time, our childish dream becomes a mature reality.

Once I had experienced full contact with the inner self and the feeling of vibrant well-being, I was able to recreate it later at will. That feeling of self-transcendence became the model for a type of meditation. Standing upright, since that is how it first happened, with my eyes wide open, I focused my mind on my inner self and let vibrating feelings of energy rise up my body to my head, then above my head. Tingling sensations up and down my spine, which became a constant purr and then pushed into my brain, announced the arrival of the completely altered state. I found that this profound contact with the inner self—and its accompanying feeling of well-being—served well as the initial stage of psychic awareness.

I had read, as you may have, that alpha brain waves accompany meditative states. Indeed, simply closing the eyes brings on alpha (ten to fourteen cycles per second) waves. Yet here I was with my eyes wide open and feeling tingling sensations in my brain. When I had an opportunity to have this transcendent state monitored by an electroencephalograph, the brainwave tracings showed the largest amplitude alpha waves the researcher had ever seen. Something interesting was going on in my head. But the same kind of tinglings were present at other centers of the body, and they could not easily be measured.

Over the years there have been surges, fluctuations, temporary losses and diminished psychic capability, and other times of heightened capability. But, finally, on April 9, 1981, something strange happened. I seemed to open up a new brain circuit in my frontal lobes. I felt a surging band of energy vibrating back and forth between the lobes. It took a few weeks to fine-tune this new capability but essentially I seemed to make a direct contact with the inner self and began to channel information directly from the inner self. I generated a number of predictions with great ease. One of the first predictions I received was that the space shuttle *Columbia*'s launch would be postponed from its scheduled April 10 takeoff. I telephoned *The New York Times* to register the prediction, and estimated a time for the postponement. I was off forty-six minutes.

This profound contact with the inner self seemed to stabilize and was accompanied by certain physiological adjustments. I found I needed far less sleep, I seemed to enjoy everything more and felt more at ease with myself than before—even food seemed to taste better—and somehow I was finding time to accomplish as much in one day as it formerly took me a week to do. My creative energies seemed considerably strengthened and new ideas began popping into my head with astonishing speed. Suddenly, life became a lot easier.

I wondered, too, if somehow I were becoming brighter. My thinking seemed to speed up and answers flashed easily into my head when questions were asked. Even my sense of humor seemed to be heightened. I seemed to be fulfilling a prediction from my last book, *Incredible Coincidence*: "Might we have within our brains unactivated circuits that will come into operation when needed?"

This experience of transformation did not, I believe, happen all by itself. It happened in the context of trying to push for greater and greater accuracy in sensing time and the future. When I pushed hard enough, it opened a new pathway of the mind. It opened a door to my inner self.

The traditional doorway for making contact with the inner self is meditation. When the mind learns to focus attention and quiet distracting chatter from the left brain, an altered state of consciousness arises which can be productive of future sight. Once the mind is trained to focus attention, meditation is no longer necessary when attempting to receive psychic impressions.

How will you know when you find that state of consciousness? When your impressions, feelings, visual imagery, and verbal messages from the inner self correspond to an outer—or future—reality. When you are able to describe something unknown to you and it turns out to be right, you know you are not imagining things. It is, by definition, extrasensory perception.

In the real world, ESP is not sharply defined and distinct from other types of knowing. Logic, intuition, guessing, hunches all play a part in coming up with the right answer. Since most of my work is now in the real world, I no longer call mysef a "psychic" but an "intuitive"—since the answers may come in many ways. The important thing is to get the right answer.

This is how my intuitive state of consciousness feels: an overall feeling of exhilaration, which is, however, kept in check; a tingling in my forehead, pronounced more on the right side; a feeling of pulsation in my solar plexus combined with a mild excited feeling, as if anticipating something pleasant; above all, an attitude of expectancy that something useful will pop into my head. When this state of consciousness becomes more profound, such a strong feeling of well-being and joy floods over me that it provokes a smile. My senses become heightened and emotions are more deeply felt.

In this state of mind it becomes easier to generate a flow of imagery in the mind's eye. Impressions, both verbal and visual, come quickly in response to questions. Sometimes the answers are specific; at other times they are symbolic.

Hypnosis is a related state of consciousness that is productive of heightened ESP perception. Over the years I have been hypnotized many times in psychic experiments, but I am coming to believe that the main effect of hypnosis is to give one permission to accomplish the impossible. It operates more on one's belief system than it does on actual production of ESP. Once you believe in your own psychic abilities, hypnosis is no longer necessary; if you can predict your future under hypnosis, you can do it while completely awake.

In reviewing my experiences in making contact with the inner self—through spontaneous uprushes, crises, meditation, hypnosis—I find I prefer the quiet, meditative approach. It is far less painful and works more productively to integrate the ways of the inner self with the conscious self. It is also more productive of future sight.

RESTRICTIONS

In talking with about a hundred psychics and others who have experienced precognition, I have concluded that the inner self puts restrictions on what may be foreseen. An anecdote told me by a Dutch writer illustrates this restriction.

In the 1950s, when the writer was researching a book on the Dutch psychic Gerard Croiset—probably the world's most gifted precognitive psychic—the writer was approached by an Italian casino who wanted to try psychic prediction as an experiment at the horse races. So the writer, Croiset and the casino owner journeyed to a race track near Paris for the experiment. Croiset extracted a promise from the casino owner that he would not bet on any of Croiset's predictions. That condition met, Croiset took a racing program and checked off his choices for the winners in seven races. Against astronomical odds, all seven horses came in.

The casino owner was stunned. He proposed that they stay one more day and repeat the experiment. Croiset said, "Now promise you won't bet."

"I won't bet," promised the casino owner.

The next morning, as before, Croiset checked off his choices for seven races. The first horse lost. The second horse lost. When the third horse came in a loser, Croiset turned to the casino owner and said, "You bet, didn't you?"

"Yes, I bet. I'm sorry. I just couldn't resist," confessed the casino owner.

The inner self puts *moral restrictions* on psychic perception. Money, like experience, must be earned. Others have told me of winning at the track or other gambling situations, but usually the winning amounted to exactly what they needed—and not a dollar more. I have never heard of multimillionaire psychics who made it by gambling. When greed becomes the motivation for use of psychic talents, the talents disappear.

CONTACT WITH THE FUTURE

In formal experiments in time, the late Gerard Croiset was without peer. Professor W.H.C. Tenhaef in Holland, Professor Hans Bender in Germany, and Dr. Jule Eisenbud in the United States were his chief investigators in analyzing chair tests. A chair test is a prediction experiment in which the subject attempts to describe in detail a person whose seat number will be chosen at random at a public hall. A number of Croiset's chair tests have been quantitatively analyzed to give high odds against chance. On a qualitative level they are impressive because of the amount of accurate detail Croiset was able to foresee about the target persons.

Important for us, though, is how Croiset made contact with those unknown persons. I believe it was through Croiset's own future experience of making contact with them at the final stage of the chair test, when the people whose numbers were drawn came up on the stage to listen to a tape recording of Croiset's predictions. Croiset had to be there, too.

This first occurred to me when I witnessed a chair test in

Zurich, Switzerland, on May 6, 1968. I had been present a few days before when Croiset recorded his predictions in Freiburg, Germany. Croiset complained that there was going to be confusion. He described a woman and included such details as her stealing a plant from someone's garden and that someone smashing a window in her home. Then Croiset began to talk about a man who did judo and was over six feet tall. Yet only *one* number was to be chosen at this experiment.

In Zurich the target person was chosen by randomly drawing counters from a basket; it turned out to be the woman Croiset had described. She visibly blushed when the recording revealed her secret about the plant theft and swift retribution. But then a man jumped up on the stage and began to translate Croiset's shaky German into more proper German. At this point the recording switched to the description of the six-footer who did judo. It was the man who had jumped on stage.

It became evident that Croiset could have given the same information if he were just asked to describe someone whom he would meet on the evening of May 6, 1968. All that shuffling of random numbers to come up with the target person was beside the point. Croiset was making contact with his own future—getting feedback to his psychic responses.

In January 1969, Croiset was filmed in Holland while he made predictions about two people who were to be chosen by a complex random system at a hall in Denver, Colorado, a few weeks later. He described a woman who had an emotional experience dealing with page 64 of a book she was reading. His description of a man included the unusual detail of his having a coat with green spots caused by a chemical from his work in a scientific laboratory.

A few weeks later in Denver, Jule Eisenbud advertised for potential target people by offering a free lecture and experiment in ESP. Those who made it through a snowstorm that night were all given questionnaires to fill out in response to Croiset's statements. Then the random selection was made. The target woman had been upset by page 64 of a book that discussed putting cats to sleep. The target man's lab coat did indeed have spots on it. Ordinarily the spots were not visible, but in the special light he used in his lab, the spots glowed green.

Eisenbud had the Denver proceedings filmed and added the Dutch footage for a film that he has available for rental. Croiset saw the film three months after it was made and received feedback on his predictions. He made contact with his future.

Let us set up some optimal situations in which we can practice prediction. There is only one caveat: Do not be afraid of making mistakes. The worst you can be is wrong.

EXERCISES

Psychometry or Object Reading

1. Find someone to act as a target person. It should be a stranger or someone you don't know well. You might meet at a dinner party, waiting at an airport, or at a doctor's office. Tell your target person that you are practicing developing your ESP. The target person should respond to your statement with a simple yes or no about their accuracy. Ask the target person for some object to hold—a watch, a ring, a comb, a wallet; or simply touch the person if that situation is comfortable. Make sure you will not be disturbed.

2. Begin your reading by telling the person what you have already learned about him or her. This gets the logical information out of the way. Now open your mind to anything at all—pictures, words, symbols—and tell the person what you see and hear. After these initial impressions, ask yourself: what sort of work does the person do, what are his or her family members like, where does the

person live, what is his or her emotional life like now? As you talk, pay attention to the imagery forming in your mind's eye. If you are beginning to "get hot," the person will agree to some of your statements. If you are wrong, shift the line of self-questioning. If you are correct in some of your statements, you are getting tuned in to the person and can proceed to the future.

3. Now ask the target person if he or she has any questions about events in his or her future. It should be something fairly important to the person, objective in nature, and not far away in time. Now you may want to attempt additional predictions if you feel you are in contact with the target person. Ask the person to telephone you when the outcome of the future event is known.

The Mysterious Stranger

1. The next time you plan to meet with a stranger (a blind date would be perfect), try to picture in your mind's eye what the stranger will look like. Sketch the person. What color eyes and hair does he or she have. Any predominant facial features? How tall? How will he or she be dressed? What is his or her personality like? Ask yourself questions about the stranger—the same questions you will ask when you meet in person.

2. When you finally meet the stranger, compare your impressions of his or her appearance with the way he or she looks. Now engage the person in conversation and ask the very questions you asked yourself earlier. Find out if any of your impressions are accurate. Mention that you are reading a book on prediction. If the stranger seems interested, you might want to reveal your precognitive impressions and sketch. If the person is not interested, do not mention your little experiment. The advantage of this exercise over many others is that the mysterious stranger never need know that he or she was the object of a psychic experiment. And if you are wrong, the person will never know!

CHAPTER 6

GUIDING IMAGES

From our dreams, meditations, and spontaneous uprushes we receive glimpses of our future—guiding images from our inner self. These guiding images come to sustain us when we reach a crossroads of life and must make a major decision that will direct the course of our future. By making an effort to understand our guiding images—and acting on them—we can fulfill our destiny.

GUIDING DREAMS

My first guiding dream came to me when I was becoming interested in psychic and spiritual development. I was wondering if it might be possible to pursue a career in parapsychology. Where might it lead? The answer came in a dream of January 26, 1966:

A TRIP IN A ROCKET SHIP
I was graduating from high school and, for my excellence, was awarded a trip in a rocket ship. I was concerned about

the propulsion system—I didn't want to go in it until I found out what made it go.

To get to the rocket ship I had to cross a bridge. There were three lanes, one wide, one medium, and one narrow. I took the narrow one on the left; it was very bumpy. Two others and I went across in a toboggan. We had to hold on very tightly, and the ride was very bumpy. At the end of the slide we crashed into a bookcase, from which fell out some books. One fell into my lap—it explained the propulsion system. I felt elated.

Attempting to interpret the dream, I wrote down possible meanings of the symbols: "The high school represents basic learning about life. The rocket ship is higher knowledge. The propulsion system may equal the spiritual force of higher knowledge. The bridge represents the paths leading to knowledge. A decision must be made to choose one. The left, narrow lane is the most difficult—dangerous but the fastest. I shall have to undergo many difficulties, perhaps fearing for my own sanity. The book on propulsion stands for wisdom and understanding of spiritual forces. I shall finally, even dramatically, find it."

The dream guided me into explorations of consciousness and seemed to be fulfilled many years later. Looking back on the dream, I can see more easily how it symbolically forecast my adventures in parapsychology. My concern about not wanting to go on the rocket ship before learning about the propulsion system accurately described my attitude of wanting to know the theoretical basis for precognition. There was also a literal element, since I learned much in making a series of predictions about the rocket ships sent to the moon in the Apollo missions. I closely identified with space exploration, and even gave my high-school graduating ambition in life as "Being the first man on the moon."

The fast, bumpy ride with two others that ended with a book accurately forecast my personal psychic experiences and laboratory work, which I wrote up in collaboration with two others in the book *Dream Telepathy*. It proposed theoretical ideas on psychic functioning, which I took further in my later books, *Patterns of Prophecy* and *Incredible Coincidence*, to develop a general theory of psychic phenomena and the underlying principles of precognition. When I visited the Manned Spacecraft Center in Houston five years after the dream, Apollo 14 astronaut Edgar Mitchell let me play out my dream in a trip in a training capsule for the Apollo missions.

For me, the importance of the dream lay not so much in any literal correspondences with the future but in the inspiring images that guided me and helped me make the major decision to enter parapsychology. The dream convinced me that my life's fulfillment could be reached by investigation of the theoretical principles that power higher knowledge. It also warned me that a bumpy ride was ahead. I soon left my job as a science editor and embarked on a voyage through time in search of that dream.

How might you recognize a guiding dream when it comes? First, consider the context of your life. If you are feeling dissatisfied or sensing that life no longer holds the excitement and challenge it once did, it may mean that you are about to make a major change. It may come when you have a major decision to make and when you call up your dream tiger for guidance.

Some characteristics of guiding dreams include positive emotion, especially at the dream's conclusion, symbolic imagery that has both a universal and personal meaning, and a goal that promises fulfillment.

A parapsychological colleague and friend, Jeffrey Mishlove, told me how a guiding dream put him on his present path. In 1980 Mishlove was awarded a Ph.D. in parapsychology by the University of California at Berkeley. It was a long and arduous study program. Mishlove even had to create his own interdisciplinary parapsychology faculty, transferring from the Department of Criminology. This major change in Mishlove's life direction began when he called up his dream tiger:

> In 1972, while I was a student in criminology at the University of California, I was also a conscientious objector—and in desperate need (I then believed) of finding alternative service work to fulfill my draft requirement. This was hard to find and was causing me a great deal of worry. My life, as a whole, seemed very unsettled at the time.
>
> In order to resolve this dilemma, I decided to program a dream to provide me with an answer.
>
> I dreamed that I went to visit some friends who lived in married student housing at Berkeley. They were not home, but knowing where they kept the key, I found it and let myself in. On the floor of the living room was a magazine called *Eye*, which I picked up and looked through. It was in that magazine, I dreamed, that I would find the answer to my problems.
>
> So the very next morning I got up and jogged over to my friends' apartment at married student housing. They were not home, but finding the key I let myself in. There, in the middle of the living room floor, was a magazine, *Focus*, the publication of KQED, a listener-sponsored radio and television station in San Francisco. It provided a focus for me, as I had the sudden realization while reading it that I would like to find alternative service work in listener-sponsored, educational media.
>
> I found a job at KPFA-FM in Berkeley, the oldest listener-sponsored radio station in the United States. Within three weeks, I was given my own biweekly radio program, *The Mind's Ear*, which opened many doors for me. My life felt together, centered. I had found my place in the universe.

Mishlove's next radio program was called *Roots of Consciousness*, for which he interviewed parapsychologists and consciousness researchers. Next he wrote a book of the same title, and that was the first stage toward getting his doctorate in parapsychology. He is now teaching parapsychology at John F. Kennedy University in Orinda, in the San Francisco Bay Area, and was recently elected president of the New Ways of Consciousness Foundation, now Spectrum Foundation.

Mishlove's guiding dream provided a literal precognition of his finding the *Focus* magazine (instead of *Eye*, which focuses). The paranormal impact of this find led him to consider deeply what answer the magazine might suggest. If he had not had the dream predicting finding the magazine, he might have just leafed through it and not thought about it.

The guiding dream may not give the answer directly but may point to where it can be found. Note how the life event, like a dream, symbolically stated that Mishlove would find *focus* in his life.

Editor-publisher Eleanor Friede, who has her own imprint with Delacorte Press, told in an interview in *Psychic* magazine how a dream provided the answer to her question about a major career change in 1971. As a newly appointed editor at Macmillan, with publicity experience, she was asked by Macmillan to reorganize and head the publicity department for a while. Not wanting to return to publicity work, she agonized over the decision for two weeks.

The day before her answer was due she had a vivid dream in which she saw herself happy as a lark, with an enthusiastic staff and a bank of offices in a special corner section. She awoke happy and reported in to accept the position.

Shortly, the department was moved to a different floor. "It was the exact corner in my dream, the same layout and number of people, with bright lights and all," she recalls. "I think now I really saw my successor, and that I was a necessary force to put her there. It was a right move, which I didn't know until I saw it in the dream."

Typical of guiding dreams, Eleanor Friede's dream not only gave her the guidance she sought but also previsioned some actual details of the future once she acted on her dream's advice. When I visited her at her dreamed-of corner office at Macmillan in 1972, she told me of many other intuitive, psychic experiences that had given her the conviction that she should follow her dreams.

Friede's most celebrated accomplishment in the book trade was signing a little book that many other publishers had rejected. At Macmillan the other editors teased her about "Friede's Folly." *Publishers Weekly* dismissed it as "ickypoo." But Friede was determined to follow her intuition and guided the book into stratospheric sales of more than twenty-four million copies around the world. Richard Bach's *Jonathan Livingston Seagull* had originally come to the writer in a series of dreamlike experiences, and in reality became the the biggest seller since *Gone with the Wind*. Both Friede and Bach were following their dreams.

TAPPING THE BLUEPRINTS OF LIFE

Even as dreams tap our deep inner self for guiding images, psychics can tap the guiding images of our lives, revealing to us future possibilities we may be unaware of or are unsure of. The important thing for us is to evaluate those images to determine if they are truly guiding images or if they come from *strongly held fantasies*.

When I undertook a series of experiments with British mediums in 1967–68, my first wife, Iris, often accompanied me and took notes of their predictions. Since she was there, the psychics often predicted events for her as well as for me. They were often uncanny in telling her she would do exactly what she held strong fantasies about: becoming an opera singer. Not a single prediction made for Iris ever came true.

As she realizes now, she had neither the vocal equipment nor the dedicated determination needed for becoming an opera personality. The psychics were not tapping her deep inner self but were merely feeding back to her strongly held fantasies of her conscious mind. Iris had determined to become an opera singer as a child of five, and the goal was reinforced when a friend of hers signed a contract with the Metropolitan Opera. But now Iris has achieved a scaled-down version of her dream: she reviews opera.

The British mediums' predictions for me, on the other hand, often did come true. Usually their predictions surprised me because I had no conscious plans or wishes in that regard, but when I heard the predictions—the ones that were later fulfilled—they felt right. They seemed to be guiding images toward which I could work. The predictions included these major points of my life: I would move to California and write for a magazine on psychic phenomena; I would become a lecturer and teacher; I would write books on psychic phenomena, including one co-authored by two others; I would develop my own psychic and healing abilities; I would do radio broadcasting (over 250 radio shows so far); I would establish an organization dealing with psychic matters (I established the New Ways of Consciousness Foundation).

For me those predictions became guiding images, and when opportunities arose for going in those directions, I seized them. They were congruent with the images of my life's blueprints, and became self-fulfilling prophecies.

ARTIFICIAL DREAMING

I have an exercise called *artificial dreaming* for those who have trouble remembering their dreams. It has proved a popular class exercise. An artificial dream is a psychic reading for someone, cast in the form of a dream or a fairy tale: It tells a story, it has symbolic meanings, it can be illogical and cut to new scenes without explanation. Since it is meant to be prophetic, the artificial dream is cast in the present and future, and emphasizes the positive aspects of life. The artificial dreamer casts the person dreamed about as the hero or heroine of the story and engages in the creative act of storytelling—which also engages ESP.

When artificial dreaming is done for someone else, there is often a mixture of the storyteller's projection and ESP about the protagonist—sometimes revealing guiding images. It is also a great deal of fun for the person making up the story. Since getting started is the hardest part, I recommend that the storyteller begin with a children's tale, since archetypal qualities suit such tales to universal symbolism. Afterward, the person dreamed about can sort out the symbolism and discover what guiding images may be present in the artificial dream.

I also suggest that people make up artificial dreams for themselves. By getting caught up in the creative act of storytelling and depending on symbols, they are able to get around the logical mind to tap guiding images from the inner self. Once the story gets underway images begin to appear in the mind's eye and the story tells itself, often wandering far from its beginning.

Here is an artificial dream I made up for myself at a recent workshop just before Easter:

THE SECRET OF TIME

I become Jack in the Beanstalk. I plant a seed in the ground and one night the full moon shines on it and a great beanstalk grows through the clouds. I climb up the beanstalk and poke my head through the little cloud. To my surprise I find a dozen golden eggs. I find a basket and put the golden eggs in the basket. I look around now and expect to see a castle and a giant. I don't see a castle. But far in the distance is a beautiful tower. As I get closer I find it is the tower of time.

As I approach the tower of time, I see a little door at the base. There is a turnstile, and I must deposit one of my golden eggs for admission. I do this and climb one story. There is another turnstile, and so I deposit another golden egg. In this way I climb eleven stories and deposit eleven eggs. When I reach the top of the tower of time, I find a special niche that is just right for the last golden egg.

When I put the final golden egg in place in the niche, there is a fanfare of trumpets and drums. The face of time becomes alive and says, "You may now ask any question."

"What is the secret of time?" I ask.

The clock face smiles and says, "Time will tell." I start laughing.

There was an interesting correspondence to an event the very next day when my family went to visit the Galleria in Glendale so that our small children could see the Easter bunny. On top of the Easter bunny's pavilion were about a dozen giant eggs. At the other end of the gallery (which I had never before visited) was a beautiful clock tower, which had an uncanny resemblance to the tower of time in my artificial dream.

Symbolically, the twelve golden eggs represent the twelve chapters of this book. Perhaps when we reach the eleventh story, or chapter, we shall find the secret of time.

BECOMING ONE ANOTHER

Sometimes we see ourselves most clearly through the eyes of another. If you have ever had the impulse to tell someone, "If I were you, I would . . ." then you will recognize the advantage of temporarily becoming someone else. This popular exercise in future consciousness could not be simpler. Two people who do not know much about each other are paired off and each assumes the identity of the other. Taking turns, about ten minutes apiece, each person introduces himself or herself in this new identity and talks about the things that are important to him or her. Then the other person questions him or her about attitudes and goals in life.

Let's say our two people are Sue and Mack. Mack says, "My name is Sue. I'm married, I work in a stationery store, but I would rather be an artist. Work at the store bores me but when I think of creating my own designs, I get excited. . . ."

The real Sue, now the pseudo-Mack, might say, "Sue, that's very interesting. Do you think you really have any talent or is this just a pipe dream because you're so bored?"

Mack, the pseudo-Sue, might answer: "I think I really do have talent, but I haven't done much with it. Maybe it's because I devote so much time to my family that I just haven't found the time to do things *I* want to do—"

And so on. The dialogue can reveal not only attitudes, situations, and talents but can also sometimes help someone discover true guiding images. By attempting to look at yourself through someone else's eyes—someone who must be using ESP if he says correct things about you—a new perspective gives much food for thought, and occasionally, flashes of enlightenment. The becoming-one-another exercise can also be fun, since it engages creative ability, acting ability, and, ideally, psychic ability.

As with the artificial dreaming exercise, it is up to you to discern what might be projection from the other person and what might truthfully apply to you. Often you will find that the other person will be most accurate when the two of you are alike in some respect. People who try this tell me that they find it unusually stimulating and they really learn some new things about themselves.

The best results from such exercises come when people are able to merge consciousness with each other. If you are successful at getting accurate imagery about the other person, it means that you have been able to suppress your own sense of ego and assume the identity of the other person. You become one with them. It is in this state of communal consciousness that you will best be able to tap the other person's inner self for the guiding images he needs.

SIFTING THE FALSE FROM THE TRUE

False images of our future arise from our ego needs and masquerade as images from the inner self. Daydreams of power, wealth, fame, success, sexual conquests, and so on—you recognize them—have a way of insinuating themselves into our predictions for ourselves. They are also the stock-in-trade of the fortune-teller who knows that a satisfied client is one who is told what he or she wants to hear.

By the time a person has reached his forties, he has experienced enough ups and downs to be wary of such false images. A mature person knows from personal experience that daydream images don't work—their allure is false. But younger people still have these lessons to learn. They are very much in the process of discovering who they are and who they will be. They are learning to sift the false images of self—which are dictated by parents, educators, and society's daydreams—from the true guiding images of their inner self that can bring them fulfillment.

To hasten this process of self-understanding, I offer some guidelines for sifting false from true predictions about oneself. I have fooled myself often enough to be sensitive to these questions:

1. Does your prediction solve all your problems at one stroke? Do you foresee that you will win the Irish sweepstakes, inherit a fortune, write the nation's number one best-seller, be a rock star, be a movie star, win the Nobel

Prize, marry a millionaire, find a gold mine, or any of a thousand other things you may have heard about that have made other people rich, famous, or successful at one stroke? If so, your prediction is probably wrong. You are conjuring up a false image from society's daydreams.

2. Does your prediction include a lot of *ifs*? If so, it is probably drawn from your ego-centered logical mind, which is forever scheming about future possibilities by computing hoped-for odds and calculating optimum chances. There is no *if* about true guiding images; they are not conditional. They just *are*.

3. Is your prediction borrowed from someone else's life? Did a friend accomplish something, and now you want to as well? Does your prediction fulfill your parents' hopes for you? Although we sometimes are inspired to follow the example of others, we must discover whether or not their guiding image is truly ours. More often than not, what works for them will not work for us, because we have our own personal destiny and our own personal guiding images.

4. Would the fulfillment of your prediction give you great satisfaction because you have worked for it? If so, it is probably a true guiding image, provided that you are the sole judge of your satisfaction and do not depend on others to give you recognition.

5. Does your prediction of some hoped-for goal depend on many others for fulfillment? The more people you must depend on to fulfill your prediction, the less likely it is a true guiding image. True guiding images tend to project only what *you* must do; how others may help rarely figures in. However, do not rule out that hoped-for goal. Once you begin fulfilling your part of the prediction, you may find that others begin to help you.

6. Do you have the talents and inner resources to fulfill your prediction? If you answer yes because you have already tested those talents and have already shown those

inner resources, your prediction is probably drawn from a true guiding image. If you cannot think of a single time during which those talents or resources manifested themselves, you may have borrowed the image from someone else. If you are not sure, put them to the test as soon as possible to find out. Bear in mind that talents develop only through practice, that an inner resource is like a muscle that must be exercised before it grows strong.

7. Does your prediction include a plan for fulfillment? If the plan is a general strategy that requires work on your part, it is probably a true guiding image. If the prediction includes precise details of who is to do what and when, it probably springs from the ego-centered logical mind. Usually guiding images from the inner self concentrate on the final picture—the goal—but do not tell you exactly how to get there. That you must discover at the necessary time.

8. Does your prediction relate to an outcome that you have not thought about before but that stimulates a good feeling? If so, you are probably tapping a true guiding image. Your feelings are the true measure of your inner self's guiding images.

9. Does your prediction massage your ego at the expense of accomplishment? If you see yourself getting acclaim but have no idea what work you need to accomplish in return for that acclaim, you are probably tapping a false image.

10. Do you predict for yourself an ideal love-mate and think about only what they will do for you and how they will love you? If so, it is probably a daydream. If you foresee how you will be able to help and love them, you may be tapping a true guiding image. If you foresee both of you helping and loving each other, you may be already sharing consciousness with that person—even though you have not yet met.

11. Does your prediction give you a profound feeling of satisfaction and accomplishment when you contemplate

its fulfillment? If so, it is probably a true guiding image of your personal destiny. When your inner self seems to glow with quiet anticipation and good feelings, it is a signal that your prediction will be self-fulfilling.

12. Can anyone else tell better than you whether your self-predictions are drawn from false or true images? If you think so, think again. You are the highest authority on your life's predictions and your life's meaning. Only you can best sift your false images from the true.

EXERCISES

Analyze Your Guiding Dream

1. If you keep a dream diary or have had success at programming dreams by calling up your dream tiger, select a dream that seems to promise some hoped-for goal in life. The dream may even be a repeating dream from childhood or perhaps just a half-remembered dream that made an impression on you. The dream should have a positive ending and evoke elation or some similar emotion.

2. Translate the symbols of your dream into a basic story of your future. Does the dream seem to indicate a major change in attitudes or professional goals?

3. Might the dream symbols contain some literal elements of your future? Try to identify any important correspondences with your reality that may have already happened.

4. Are the dream symbols drawn from past experience? Were those good experiences or promising ones?

5. In your mind's eye witness the conclusion of the dream and pay attention to the emotion that is evoked. If there is a strong positive emotion, let the dream image inspire and guide you. Return to that guiding image in your

mind whenever you doubt you will get where you want to go.

Artificial Dreaming for Others

1. Find a stranger or casual acquaintance for a target person at a dinner party or some social event. Make sure you will not be interrupted. Tell that person you are going to make up a dream about his present and future, which he will have to interpret.
2. Let your imagination have free rein as you make up a story or dream about the other person. You may wish to start with some children's tale with the target person as protagonist. You are free to be as illogical as you like in your creative storytelling. Be entertaining and concentrate on positive aspects of the future as you improvise your artificial dream.
3. Now ask the target person for his interpretation. Does it make any sense to him? Does it correspond at all to the person's life situation? Are the symbols well chosen? What outcome does the artificial dream seem to predict for that person?
4. Now reverse the roles and ask the other person to make up an artificial dream for you. Give him feedback about any correct details and interpret the symbols for him. Are there symbols or themes that particularly appeal to you as possibilities in your life? Record them and later consider them in the light of the questions in the section "Sifting the False from the True."

For Yourself

1. Find an audience to whom you will tell an artificial dream for yourself. It could be one person or a group you feel comfortable with, so you can say what you feel. Using

yourself as protagonist, make up a story about your future. Regard it as an exercise in creativity—therefore you cannot be "wrong." Get caught up in the creative rush of your words and don't worry about what will come up next. Images will form in your mind's eye and show the rest of the dream to you. *Don't attempt to analyze it while you are telling the dream.* This should be an enjoyable experience for you and entertaining for your audience. Be positive.

2. With the help of your audience, try to analyze the dream. Look for themes or incidents that appeal to you. Are there any possible predictions for you? Were there surprises for you in the dream? If there seem to be guiding images, review them with the questions in the section "Sifting the False from the True."

Becoming One Another

1. Find a target person whom you do not know well. Tell that person you will play a game in which you assume each other's identity. To start, announce yourself in your new identity and say what you already know about the target person. Then say anything that pops into your head; it could be about the person's attitudes, present life situation, what he or she hopes to do in the future. Make sure that the target person knows that he can ask questions, and before long you will have a dialogue with the identities reversed.

2. Now reverse the roles and let the other person become you. Ask questions about yourself. Does the other person seem to describe you accurately? Does he give you suggestions about your future? Do you have a positive emotional reaction to some of the other person's predictions? If so, they might be guiding images.

3. Did you find that you and the target person are alike in some ways? Explore your common life situations and

attitudes. Did you gain any insights about yourself and your possible future?

Acting on It

If you discovered any true guiding images in your explorations, think about how you might act on them.

CHAPTER 7

THE ART OF PROPHECY

The prediction of public events—what I term *prophecy*—requires both psychic and logical insights. It is important to realize that one can prophesy only about possible futures.

Many prophecies are triggered by the dramatic impact of extraordinary news events, events which disrupt our emotions and stir our psyches to sense the next stages in the unfolding drama.

INTERPRETING DREAMS

When the awful news of Robert Kennedy's assassination reached me in Germany in June 1968, my personal grief was compounded because my warning premonition had not been able to prevent that tragedy. As I studied British newspaper accounts of Robert Kennedy's funeral, and a photo of his son, Joseph, then fifteen, filing past the coffin, I seemed to make psychic contact with Joseph.

The contact extended to Edward Kennedy when I read a journalist's speculations on "The Fate of the Dynasty":

> The Kennedys have become, it seems to me, a dangerous American obsession, almost an invitation, if not a provocation, to lunatic acts of violence. They have become like one of those old British families with a legendary curse on the heir. It may just be superstition, but the superstition itself induces an unhealthy atmosphere which helps to perpetuate the legend. The drama of the Kennedys and the Presidency is a play that has gone on long enough, and if Edward Kennedy tries to make a third act of it, then it really is tempting the devil.

Thousands of miles away from home, I wondered how the American people felt about the possibility of Ted Kennedy seeking the presidency. And would Joseph Kennedy become the heir to the Kennedy dynasty? Would it be cursed? On June 13, I awoke with a dream:

JFK RETURNS TO LIFE

President John Kennedy returned to life, and was again seeking the presidency. I was not a supporter, though I wasn't really against him. We waited for buses to take us to the campaign dinner. There were three places for the buses, one for each campaign. The first waiting place was very long; the other two were short. The group waiting at the last stop was so small that John decided to drive us there in his car. Three others and I then went to dinner with John Kennedy.

There was also my college classics professor, with whom I spoke of Latin. At the dinner party JFK was very charming. He gave us each something he had created. From some protoplasmic material his hand fashioned a nice piece of art. As he was taking me and another young man back to the car, I had to admit I thought he was best. The young man moved up and sat in the car to my right as if there were a seat facing sideways toward us, somewhat forward. We drove past a storefront, seemingly linked with another past campaign, but it was shut. I remember a sign, something like, "Would John F. Kennedy Make Pres . . . ident Again?"

I wrote down my interpretation of the dream symbols and my associations: "Yesterday I was wondering if the Kennedy family would one day become a ruling dynasty over America. I was (and am) somewhat hesitant about that idea. The dream seems to be precognitive and is linked with an earlier dream of June 8, in which John Kennedy's "kid brother" learns the dance of life in politics. Perhaps then Ted Kennedy will again seek the presidency. The three bus stops: the first long one represents JFK's presidency, the second short one represents Robert's campaign attempt, the third one, Ted's campaign in the future. The talk with my classics professor about Latin might be connected with his talks about the emperors of ancient Rome and the dynasties of ancient Egypt. Kennedy creating something artful and nice-looking seems a good sign indeed. The gap in the word *Pres . . . ident* means perhaps a gap between the Kennedy presidencies. The closed storefront relating to a previous campaign seems to represent Robert Kennedy's now closed campaign. The young man in the car with us may be yet another Kennedy who will be brought along into the fore (Bobby's son Joseph?). For it was with him that I noticed the closed storefront.

My first attempt at prophesying from the dream turned out to be wrong—a 1971 prediction that Ted Kennedy would be elected president in 1976. In 1979, however, when polls showed Ted Kennedy the popular favorite as the next Democratic candidate for president, I took another look at the dream and realized my mistake. The dream did not say he would *win* the presidency, only that his campaign would be short. Ted's bus stop had the fewest supporters of all. Although he had grown wise in the dance of politics and was creating something good for us, the dream seemed to predict that he would withdraw from the presidential race.

On October 23, 1979 I registered with the Central Premonitions Registry the prediction that "Senator Ted Kennedy will drop out of the presidential race in 1980." I estimated the time as "possibly around February 1980." The prediction was published in *The Star* on November 13, 1979, and contradicted the majority of presidential predictions: "According to the psychics, Ted Kennedy will be a sweep."

In February the first cries came for Kennedy's withdrawal from the presidential race, but he held on until the night before the first ballot at the Democratic convention. When Kennedy's forces lost a rules-change ballot, he officially withdrew his name from nomination.

My 1968 dream also seemed to predict that Ted Kennedy will assist in the future presidential campaign of Joseph Kennedy. If Joseph repeats the pattern of John Kennedy, it could come as early as 1996 when Joseph will be forty-three years old—the age at which John won the presidency. The final outcome was posed as a question in my dream: "Will a Kennedy make president again?"

If the dream is truly prophetic of the next stage of this drama, we can breathe a sigh of relief that there is, at least at this point, no sign of that legendary curse on the heir.

Estimating the date for the fulfillment of a prophetic dream is extremely difficult. I recently discovered, however, a relationship that might prove to be a valuable tool in working with precognitive dreams. The formula is simple: If there is an element from the past in the dream, the future event will be that many years in the future. For example, in my dream "JFK Returns to Life" there is a reference to my college classics professor and the Latin language. I took Latin in 1956 and 1957, which is eleven to twelve years before the 1968 dream; therefore (I should have realized) it predicted that Ted Kennedy would seek the presidency eleven to twelve years *after* the dream—in 1979 or 1980.

This insight into past and future dream time was triggered by the work of precognition researcher Fred Blau of Sebastapol, California. In tracing time elements from the past and future in his dreams, Blau found a symmetry between the past and future. It occurred to me that if such a symmetry exists *in the same dream*, it might prove a key to the elusive future time. In checking out already fulfilled prophetic dreams that contain datable elements from the past, I have found this relationship to hold up. But lest I be accused of relying on that famous twenty-twenty hindsight, let me make a prediction from a dream about the future with an estimate of the time.

This dream of May 25, 1970 has already had two fulfillments; let's try a prediction for a third:

> I was showing someone some poems of mine that I had only just discovered were printed in a 1959 magazine. And then I saw a new issue of *Reader's Digest* that had two poems printed, one by me and one by someone else I knew. The second one was about how we wished we could undo the past victory over Russia, for that had caused the trouble now.

The first fulfillment came in 1972 when *Reader's Digest* reprinted an article from *Psychic* magazine, on acupuncture, which I edited. The second fulfillment came in 1979 when *Reader's Digest* published an article on coincidence ("Coincidence: Is It Black Magic or Blind Chance?" by Edward Ziegler) in the August issue, which included material from my book *Incredible Coincidence* and material from books by Arthur Koestler, whom I know.

The element from the past in the dream—something printed in a magazine from 1959—reminds me of a science-fiction story I had written in high school and which was printed years later without my knowledge. Subtracting

1959 from 1970 gives eleven years; adding eleven to 1970 gives 1981. The last chapter of this book describes an ESP war with Russia (like the dream's victory over Russia) and has science-fiction elements in it (like the 1959 story). So that dream may predict that the *Reader's Digest* will reprint the last chapter of this book in 1981. Interested readers should be able to check on that prediction soon.

Repeated fulfillments from the same prophetic dream happen frequently. Keep this in mind when attempting to predict from your own dreams. If the first part of a dream is fulfilled, it is more likely that other parts of the dream will be fulfilled later. Of course if dates (or datable elements from the past) appear in the dream, subtract them from the year of the dream to get the number of years in the future the most important fulfillment will take place.

When attempting to interpret a dream about the future, you should keep in mind several basic clues:

1. If the dream itself refers to the future or the subject of precognition, it is probably prophetic.
2. Your associations to the dream elements—what they remind you of—should be considered a part of the dream.
3. Life events just before and after the dream may also be part of the prophetic experience and should be considered when making a prediction. Your associations to these life events may also be important.
4. If your dream is prophetic of some event near in time, it may also predict later fulfillments of that pattern in your life.

Here is an example of a prophetic dream from my own life. Its fulfillment was witnessed by millions of people but its significance was important mainly to me.

The experience began on March 13, 1972, while I was

writing *Patterns of Prophecy*. While puzzling over the semantic problem of precognition versus prophecy, I received a telephone call from parapsychologist Chuck Honorton, at Maimonides Dream Laboratory, about an article on precognition in *Playboy*.

Honorton told me of a dream in which he and I were appearing on the Johnny Carson show. I had had a similar dream recently. But my association to Honorton's dream was a humorous dialogue he had with my first wife, Iris, when she was a subject in an experiment. She had dreamed about Johnny Carson and David Frost, both hosts of TV talk shows. Iris kept referring to Johnny Frost. Finally, Chuck burst out laughing and said, "Jack Frost!"

That dialogue was my primary association to Honorton's dream, so I felt that the dream might refer to the *David Frost Show* instead of Johnny Carson's *Tonight Show*, which was produced on the West Coast. The *David Frost Show* was produced in New York City, where I lived then. So I registered this prediction with Robert Nelson, director of the Central Premonitions Registry: "Here's a prediction you will be able to check personally on TV. Charles Honorton and I and someone else (you?) will appear on a nationwide talk show on TV. I think it will be the *David Frost Show*. . . . Both Chuck and I have had dreams about appearing on the Johnny Carson show, but I think this is an association with the *David Frost Show*."

A few days later I was astonished to receive a telephone call from a producer of the *David Frost Show*. The show wanted to interview some parapsychologists and psychic subjects, such as myself, who worked in laboratories. Dr. Stanley Krippner, Honorton's colleague at Maimonides Dream Laboratory, had agreed to appear on the show and had recommended they contact me. Instead of Honorton, his colleague Krippner appeared on the show with me. It aired April 28, just a few weeks after my prediction. Since then Honorton has appeared on a number of national TV shows as have I and Robert Nelson.

I might add that I have since then had more dreams about meeting Johnny Carson, but I am less than confident they predict an appearance on his show since in the last dream we were arguing over a tennis game. Yet it was an amiable argument, and since I don't play tennis (but Carson does) it might indicate an attempt by me to "play his game." In fact, the dream might be completely symbolic of my hopes to become a television talk-show host.

Sometimes prophetic dreams contain a future time designation that is somewhat scrambled. For instance, two years before my son Thomas was born I had a dream in which my wife and I were worried about our boy growing too fast; he was only two years old and was already six feet tall. I construed that to mean that in two years we would have a baby boy who would grow to be quite tall. He seems to be fulfilling the prediction.

When analyzing your dreams for possible clues about time, pay attention to numbers. Play with them and see if they might be translated into prophetic time units.

In general, to make use of dreams as prophecy it is absolutely necessary to record them and review them periodically. In that way you come to know not only your dream symbols but you develop an intuitive understanding of their meaning—both for the present and the future. Most of your prophetic dreams will predict your own future. But occasionally events in your future will be newsworthy, such as the following example.

In August 1971, when I was living in New York City but planning to move to San Francisco, I recorded a dream about witnessing a minor earthquake. I published part of the dream with the prediction: "May be partially precognitive of an earthquake I shall witness one day. . . . Since I am planning to go to the West Coast, it is more logical for it to be there."

The rest of the dream described confusion over a commuter train ticket, resolved when a parapsychological colleague, Rex Stanford of Texas, found the ticket. The commuter train ticket seemed odd since I had never used one before.

Soon after I moved to San Francisco in 1973, the Bay Area Rapid Transit (BART), a commuter train, went into operation. A train commuter ticket now became a possibility. When Rex Stanford visited San Francisco on two occasions, I wondered if there would be an earthquake. Then in August 1979 the Parapsychological Association was planning its first Bay Area convention at St. Mary's College in Moraga. I was planning to attend and would have to take the BART train. Rex Stanford was planning to attend. This could be it, I thought.

On the opening day of the convention I was asked to appear on a radio program broadcast by KQED, a special series on the mind. The interviewer, Kevin Purseglove, asked me about parapsychological research and concluded his questioning by asking if I had any predictions.

"Just one," I said. "I am expecting a small earthquake in the Moraga-Orinda area where the parapsychologists are meeting—because of a dream I had eight years ago. The earthquake will have to be in the next two to three days."

Two days later, precisely at 8:43 on the morning of August 17, my San Francisco apartment twisted and jolted as I was dressing to attend the convention.

"Ah!" I exclaimed, "there's my predicted earthquake." I wasn't worried about it since my 1971 dream told me it would be minor. As it turned out, the epicenter struck one mile away from the parapsychologists' meeting place in the Moraga-Orinda area.

When I arrived at the convention, one of the first people I talked to was a parapsychologist I had met some months before in New York, Nancy Sondow. She showed me a dream she had recorded about *me*. In her dream I was having problems with a train ticket. I explained that I did indeed have my usual problems with the BART computer train ticket the day before—when she had her dream. I was intrigued because of the connection with my dream of 1971 in which a train ticket assumed so much importance for a time when there would be an earthquake with Rex Stanford around.

By noticing two of the dream's elements about to come into reality, I was able to predict the third element—the earthquake—to complete fulfillment of the eight-year-old dream. Are earthquakes set up in blueprint form many years before they happen?

That earthquake, though minor physically, seemed to assume a greater symbolic character in a report on the convention by Barbara Honegger: "Quake Hits Parapsychology: Earthshaking questions and challenges—as well as a real, live California earthquake—rumbled through this year's annual Parapsychological Association's convention seemingly setting the stage for a revolution in paranormal research."

PSYCHIC SENSING

The major media event in 1981's calendar of psychic events was the January 6 nonprediction by Tamara Rand that Ronald Reagan would be shot. On investigation by Cable News Network, it was revealed that her prediction had been taped in a television studio on March 31, the day *after* the shooting. The tape had "January 6, 1981" superimposed on it retroactively in what became the most publicized hoax of the year—rivaling the journalistic hoax about a Pulitzer Prize that had to be taken back. The media made merry with Tamara Rand. Johnny Carson quipped, "NBC finally figured out what went wrong with their season. They fired Tamara Rand as their resident psychic."

To even the score for January 6, here is a prediction I

made that day. It was registered with the Central Premonitions Registry and later with Cable News Network's *Freeman Reports*, the program that exposed Tamara Rand:

". . . the launch date (of the space shuttle *Columbia*) would be closer to *April 12* than the present schedule (March 17)."

As the world knows, the March 17 date was postponed until April 10, when a million people were waiting for the ship to blast off at the Kennedy Space Center and land at Edwards Air Base in California. A computer malfunction delayed the launch until my target date, April 12. (Other parts of that prediction will be discussed in Chapter 9.) Since the media haven't publicized *my* January 6 prediction, which the *Columbia* so ably fulfilled, it seems only fair that I do so. I make mistakes, too, but not retroactive ones. I feel no shame at being wrong, since it is something of a marvel ever to be right.

Here is a good example of an interesting mistake: On April 16, 1981, I was doing a psychic demonstration for a group and was puzzled when the name "Nashua" came in. I had no associations with the name, although the person I was talking with said it might be an attempt to get a car name, Nissan, that she had been talking to someone about a few minutes before.

Later I stopped at my neighborhood bar and was chatting with a stranger. He mentioned the Nissan brand of car. Intrigued by the coincidence, I asked him if he knew of the name Nashua. "It's a Navajo Indian word for happiness," he told me. Startled that he was familiar with the name, I made a note of it, and we talked further about his plans for opening a ranch and riding horses. When I reached home, I mentioned the incident to my wife, who said that Nashua was the name of a thoroughbred racehorse. A few days later, her brother mentioned that his choice for the Kentucky Derby was Flying Nashua. These coincidences seemed meaningful, so I registered the prediction on April 20 that "The Kentucky Derby will be won by Flying Nashua."

On May 1 and 2, Flying Nashua made the headlines of the sports pages. The horse had been denied entry to the Kentucky Derby so the owner filed a lawsuit, and the judge agreed the horse should run on May 2 in the derby. It didn't come close to winning, but it did make the headlines for my target time of the Kentucky Derby.

Over the years I have made a few sports predictions, mostly at the request of reporters, and I have found a consistent pattern in these predictions: I am always wrong. I seem unable to make psychic contact with sports events, possibly because they do not interest me. There is also the problem of moral restrictions since sports events are often the object of gambling. My inner self refuses to allow me to gamble or to contribute to gambling by others.

My strong suit is sensing future time. I study the calendar and estimate the time of future events. I get feedback and adjust my predictions on the next attempt. There is nothing metaphysical at work, only development of human talent and a great deal of practice. Typically, the raw data of psychic sensing, like dreams, do not contain specific references to future time. We must therefore devise mental calendars for time estimation. If habitually practiced, time sensing can become second nature. It is important to realize, though, that future events are not frozen in time but shift according to human free will: Some events get postponed, some never happen at all, some may even be prevented from happening.

The single greatest obstacle to accurate prophecy is emotion. If we strongly desire something to happen, our chances of prophetic success diminish. If our emotional desires, wishes, hopes, fantasies enter into our considerations when prophesying we are only projecting the future the way we want it to be, not predicting what it will be.

When emotion is expressed on a negative level, we project our worst fears and nightmares—even feelings of personal dissatisfaction and ill health—onto the world in the guise of prophecy. In my own experience I have found that a balance of great interest and emotional objectivity is the best possible attitude when undertaking a predictive task.

Emotional involvement crowds out cool professionalism when *your* life is the subject of prophecy. It takes a great deal of discipline and work to achieve an objectivity about your own future. I find the best attitude to adopt when foreseeing good things in your own life is: It's fine if it happens, but I won't count on it. I can strive mightily to *make* it happen, both physically and psychically, but I will have no cause for disappointment if it does not work out as well as I hope. Nothing in life—especially prophecy—is ever perfect.

THE PSYCHIC BANDWAGON EFFECT

The most infamous source of error in prophecy is what I call the "psychic bandwagon effect." The same source of error exists among scientific predictors but they call it "relying on expert forecasts." The files of the Central Premonitions Registry are clogged with predictions made by people who have been impressed by prophecies made by some famous psychic or scientist. People climb on the psychic bandwagon and offer additional details of the previsioned event, usually a calamity of world-shaking significance.

A good example of the psychic bandwagon effect is Paul James's book *California Superquake, 1975-1977?: Scientists, Cayce, Psychics Speak.* Inspired by Jess Stearn's 1968 best-seller on Edgar Cayce, *The Sleeping Prophet*, a small army of psychics and would-be psychics reiterated

Cayce's prediction that California would suffer such a great earthquake that it would fall into the sea. James collected their predictions and attempted to pinpoint a date—1975–1977—for this calamity. A more recent book by Jeffrey Goodman, *We Are the Earthquake Generation*, uses the same formula to predict a later date.

I believe that these earthquake predictions have absolutely no validity. Once someone—even the very best psychic—has accepted an idea logically, objectivity is lost; the logical mind takes over and masquerades as psychic intuition. For the record, Jess Stearn, who popularized the California superquake thesis, now lives on the coast of Southern California. When asked if he was worried, he replied that he felt the Cayce prediction was about the far future. One psychic source that I'm inclined to respect says that it is eight hundred years in the future. In the meanwhile, California coastal real estate should be an excellent investment.

Cayce's prophecies of a cataclysmic shifting of the earth's poles around the beginning of the third millennium first aroused my interest in 1966. Researching other sources of similar predictions for my book *Patterns of Prophecy*, I was struck by the coincidence of these parallel predictions. Taking this research further, author John White has compiled a massive collection of pole shift predictions in his book, *Pole Shift: Predictions and Prophecies of the Ultimate Disaster*. I can discount some of the recent predictions on the grounds of the psychic bandwagon effect, but there remains a residue of prophecy that makes me respectful of the concept, if skeptical of the dates. As I wrote in that book's foreword, "I, for one, will keep a careful eye out for any fulfilled predictions that are on the psychic timetable to precede the prophesied pole shift. . . . If there's something to it, we should be finding out sooner than we may like to think." I feel certain that the conscious minds of these psychics have elaborated, embroidered, exaggerated the prophetic impulses from their deep unconscious, so I dismiss the predicted details.

But a gnawing intuition makes me suspect that a possible trigger for a pole shift—the approach of some celestial body or dark star—may be a real possibility by the century's end or the next millennium's beginning. I feel no need for panic or preparations for catastrophe, but I do feel a need for more acute scientific exploration of our nearby heavens. Something is on its way—something indescribable. It will inspire awe more than terror, wonder more than fear, and have as its greatest impact on the human race a raising of consciousness that will usher in a new era of understanding. Because that statement does not make any logical sense, it must come from the unconscious. It is a prophecy, not a prediction. Perhaps in twenty years time we will be in a position to make predictions on a scientific basis about this approaching entity. In the meanwhile, we have much to learn about the scientific basis of prophecy.

To obtain reliable psychic information about large-scale future events, we must seek out data on the personal level. We must investigate and record dreams and intuitions, must inaugurate scientific study of prophetic impulses of the general populace, study premonitions that happen daily to thousands of people, compare data and fit the pieces of the puzzle of the future into place. Each of us foresees imperfectly but together we may glimpse a truer picture of tomorrow's promise—and premonition.

The more abstract an event is, the more difficult it is to predict. Only by tuning in to individuals who will partake in some future event can we rely on prophetic accuracy. In your experiments in prophecy, do not leap on the psychic bandwagon; do not attempt to predict global disasters and earthquakes. Start with something small, something that interests you, something that you can make psychic contact with but can maintain emotional objectivity about—

and above all, something that you can get feedback on soon.

When I studied with Gerard Croiset in Holland, he told me that the psychic information he received then was no better than when he had begun to do psychic work twenty years before, but through intensive study, analysis, and application of logic, he learned to extract far more meaning and accuracy out of his raw psychic data. There is just no substitute for practice, study, and discipline. Mastering the art of prophecy is like learning a foreign language: You have ten thousand mistakes to make. The faster you make them, the faster you learn.

EXERCISES

Dream Prophecy

1. If you have recorded a dream about some person whose future interests you, write out the major elements of the dream and translate them from symbols into basic themes.

2. If you do not already have such a dream, review the Exercise section in "Training Your Dream Tigers" and program a dream about some target person.

3. Does your dream refer to the future or to precognition? Do any of the dream's elements have a prophetic quality? Does the dream describe something that has not happened in the past but conceivably could happen in the future? Briefly describe what your dream might predict.

4. Now try to rule out possible personal references. Ask yourself if the target person might be a symbol for some aspect of yourself. Does the dream remind you of any current situation in your own life? Did you make contact with the target person just before the dream? If the dream does not seem drawn from your own life, and you have been

thinking about the target person, assume that your dream may be about that person's experience.

5. If there was a reference to a past event in your dream, assume that your prediction will be fulfilled in about the same distance of time in the future.

6. If your dream seems to predict the near future, and might interest the target person, share your dream with him or her and ask for feedback. If the prediction is about some well-known person, register your prediction with the Central Premonitions Registry. You may receive your feedback in the media if the event is newsworthy. If some news item does correspond with your prediction, send a copy to the CPR.

7. If your dream prediction is fulfilled in some way, study the correspondences with what actually happened. This will give you a better idea of how your individual dreaming style previsions the future.

Psychic Prophecy

1. Select as your target some scheduled future event that interests you and involves a target person whose photo is available. You can also make contact with a target person by watching him on television.

2. Touch the photo of the target person or create that person's image in your mind's eye to make psychic contact.

3. Ask your inner self to give you pictures in your mind's eye to show you the future. You may wish to speak your impressions into a tape recorder. Pay attention to images quickly flashing through your mind's eye. Do not attempt to interpret them initially, just observe them. If any words come to mind, record them also. Only after you have established a flow of imagery, sensations, and impressions should you try to ask for specific information, such as

names, places, and times. Initials are more to be trusted than full names.

4. After your impression session, analyze your images as if they were elements of a dream. Try to translate your impressions into a coherent prediction.

5. In your mind's eye create a calendar of the future and ask when the event might occur.

6. If your prediction seems at variance with what experts think or what you might have guessed, send it to the CPR.

7. When the outcome of the future event becomes known, compare your prediction with details of what happened. Did some of the images you thought were literal turn out to be symbolic? If there is a striking correspondence with your prediction, send a copy of the news item to the CPR.

CHAPTER 8

THE SCIENCE OF PREDICTION

Scientific forecasting pervades every element of our society. Computers keep the stock on our grocery shelves flowing to match demand, economists match supply and demand to predict financial outcomes, governments predict tax revenues and expenditures, the National Weather Service uses sophisticated satellites to give us odds on what the weather will be in our communities, farmers predict the yield of their crops, television prophets predict what the public will want to watch for entertainment, scientists predict the development of technological marvels, and we predict whether or not we will be able to make it to the end of the month.

Did you ever notice how wrong such "scientific" forecasting can be? The radio announcer predicts clear weather while you watch the rain out your window. The government runs out of money again because economic forecasters were wrong about increased revenues. The most highly touted television shows, which market research predicted would be big winners, come and go in six weeks, practically unviewed.

The trouble with scientific forecasting is that it assumes a surprise-free scenario of the future, whereas the future keeps hitting us with surprises.

We have gotten used to these surprises sufficiently well enough not to be shocked at them any more. What is shocking is that scientific predictors do not realize that many "surprises" can be foreseen. Scientific forecasting is thought of by scientists as the only way to see the future. It's about time that forecasters began to use the right half of their brain to achieve a true science of prediction. When the two halves of the brain, logic and intuition, are combined, we are able to forecast on solid empirical data *and also* intuit some of those surprises.

LOGIC AND INTUITION

Give two experts with the same background the same scientific data and ask them to predict the outcome, and you will get two different answers. One man's logic is another man's wild fantasy. The man with the greater scientific training is not necessarily the better prophet.

A friend who trained Orky, the 14,000-pound killer whale at Marineland in Palos Verdes, California, recently told me how intelligent his remarkable performer is. He described a feat he had taught Orky and asked me to estimate how long it took the animal to learn it. I said I had no idea. He urged me to guess. "Four minutes," I said.

"That's not fair," my friend complained. "You got the answer psychically. Any expert trainer would have said four to six weeks. It took Orky actually about three and a half minutes."

Lacking any expertise in my friend's area of knowledge,

I merely listened to whatever words popped into my head. But I honestly cannot say if what I said was psychic, intuitive, or just a good guess. The important thing was that my answer was right—or at least better than informed expertise might have given.

We all have the ability to come up with the right answer—if we are not seduced by the notion that logic takes precedence over intuition. How many times have you begun to answer some question off the top of your head correctly, only to find yourself saying, "Oh, that *can't* be right because—[logical reason]." Intuitions are often vague, but they carry a conviction of rightness for those who have learned to listen to them. Someone who learns to balance logic and intuition to predict the future should be enormously successful—especially in making major business decisions. Strong statistical support for this statement was gathered by two researchers at the Newark College of Engineering. When Douglas Dean and John Mihalasky gave precognition tests to company presidents, it was discovered that the successful presidents (those who had doubled their company profits in the last five years) scored above chance. Unsuccessful company presidents scored below chance. The precognition test—a computer card that would later have a hundred numbers chosen by random chance—was particularly well designed for businessmen since numbers are the bottom line in business. In their book, *Executive ESP*, Dean and Mihalasky offer fascinating stories of how financial wizards use their intuition to make bids that undercut the competition by a few hundred dollars when millions are at stake. The right numerical answer can come only through intuitive, psychic processes. But the businessman has to be expert in logical understanding and manipulation of numbers as well. It is mostly at the top management level that decisions must be made for which insufficient data are available for logical analysis. Should we drill an oil well at location X? Should we merge with company B? Should we acquire company Y? Should we bid on contract C, and how much?

Questions like these are successfully answered by intuitive company presidents. The results of their decisions will not be known for a long time. What seems like a *logical* decision today may turn out to have a bad outcome tomorrow; what seems like an *illogical* decision today may have the best outcome in the future. All company presidents must demonstrate a high level of logical ability, but it is those who can also tap their intuitive, psychic abilities who will best foresee the "surprises" that make the most lucrative business deals.

A company president or financial wizard seldom brags about his or her intuition or ESP supplying the right answer. Rather, he or she manufactures a logical-sounding excuse for this foreknowledge. The financial community still regards ESP as kooky and distrusts the unknown. But when a chairman of the board retires, we hear the true stories of how he or she made millions for the company through hunches and intuition.

Shortly after he retired as chairman of the board of Phillips (66) Petroleum, William W. Keeler admitted that many of his successes came from paying attention to inner feelings. "There were too many incidents that couldn't be explained merely as coincidences. I had successes in uncharted areas. My strong feelings toward things were accurate—when I would let myself go."

Pointing to his solar plexus, Keeler said, "I get to feeling it right here, and it is very strong. In fact, it sometimes is so strong I think of it as fact."

In one extraordinary example, Keeler told how he was able to project an engineering graph curve with only one data point. "I saw an instantaneous value for pressure, temperature, and catalysis at one particular point, yet I can't tell you why or how I got it."

My analysis for why: He needed the information. For

how: His intuitive gut feeling worked its way up to his mind's eye to emerge as a full-scaled psychic impression with accurate details.

Keeler's experience typifies the balanced logical and intuitional brain functioning characteristic of scientific genius. Intent focus of attention on a problem combined with expert knowledge makes the sudden leap to the right answer in a flash of awareness that bypasses logical processes. *Eureka!* Afterward comes the studied application of logic to discover if the answer is indeed correct; the hows and whys must now be sought; testing must be done; ways to prove or disprove the instant insight require hard work of the logical mind.

Science textbooks present the path of discovery and knowledge as proceeding from diligent logic and sound thinking. But that's a cover-up. What really happens is that the answer comes first by creative, intuitional, and psychic means, and the logical pathways to it are created later. One true case of scientific brilliance, however, is finally making it into the texts: Einstein discovered the principle of relativity at age sixteen in an intuitive image in his mind's eye and then spent many years trying to prove it.

If our educational system tried to encourage creative and brilliant thinking, teachers would not reprimand Johnny for "not paying attention" but would ask him, "Johnny, what insights did you have just now while you were in your right-brain mode?"

Johnny's periods of "not paying attention" happen about every ninety minutes, in the same rhythm as nocturnal dreams. Daydreams are closely linked to right-brain functioning, including intuition and ESP. In other words, daydreaming is conducive to future consciousness. Like nocturnal dreams, daydreams serve our primary needs from the unconscious but also scan our environment for future events that threaten or interest us. We can artificially induce dreams to provide pictures and words about the future. If we call our artificial dreams "visions of the future," we are in the business of futurology.

LOOKING FORWARD

People who write their visions of the future in an entertaining, dramatic, and vivid style are called science-fiction writers. People who document their scenarios of the future by research and who logically argue their visions are called scientific experts or futurists. Sometimes the two breeds are mixed, as in the person of Arthur C. Clarke, who writes both fiction and nonfiction predictions. In his 1958 study of the prophetic accuracy of both schools of prediction, *Profiles of the Future*, Clarke found that science-fiction writers, using their creative, intuitive approach, were far more accurate than their logical scientific brethren in forecasting dates of technological progress. As it turned out, both schools of prediction overestimated the arrival times of future technologies. The marvels of tomorrow were here before anyone predicted they would be. The lesson should have been clear: Intuition is superior to logic in prediction.

Clarke's own combination of logic and intuition has produced some excellent prophetic hits: In 1947 he predicted that the first rocket ship would land on the moon in 1959—a direct hit with the first Russian unmanned moon launch. He was only off by five months with his 1958 prediction of a manned moon landing in 1970 (Apollo 11 landed on July 20, 1969).

Witlessly unheeding Clarke's studies, a California think tank, the Rand Corporation, devised the Delphi technique in which they asked scientists instead of science-fiction writers to predict future dates of scientific breakthroughs. Rand averaged these predicted dates to arrive at a projection for the most probable date. To show you how silly this can get, the most improbable event of a 1967 study—to happen between the years 2020 and never—was "use of telepathy and ESP in communications."

Right here in 1981—long before never—we have reliable use of ESP both in the laboratory and in real-life experiments, such as the use of psychic teams to discover archaeological finds. Admittedly, the emphasis on the use of ESP is not in communications fields—we have reliable electronic means for most uses—but on uses that have no counterpart in the world of machines, such as precognition and remote viewing. Nor is that use widespread in the scientific community. But it is available.

If the Rand Corporation wants a technique that works in arriving at accurate predictions of technological developments, all they need do is take the *least conservative* estimate and discard the rest. And it would help their track record if they asked a few psychics and science-fiction writers for their predictions.

Happily, *The Book of Predictions* does include predictions by science-fiction writers and a handful of psychics as well as scientific experts. Only two of the book's predictors mention psychic abilities: Beverly Jaegers of St. Louis and me. I recently had the opportunity to meet Ms. Jaegers and discovered that we have much in common. We both began in research and teaching and both developed our psychic abilities in research situations. It turns out that we have nearly identical predictions for the use of psychic abilities:

Jaegers: "Parapsychology will become an accepted subject at all major universities. Psi labs will be set up in leading cities to combat the threat of Soviet psionics, which will be in the world's headlines in the 1980s, and to explore this newest evolution of man and his mind."

Vaughan: "The United States will start a massively

funded program in psychic research in an attempt to catch up with Soviet advances. Like the Soviet program, the American psychic program will be developed by the military."

It is perhaps no chance coincidence that both Jaegers and I predict the same date for these events: 1984. In our discussion about our nearly identical predictions, we both referred to logical facts and psychic surmise. We also felt that the U.S. government would keep its head in the sand until it was too late.

In my years of research in evaluating predictions, I concur with Arthur C. Clarke that scientists are most conservative, science-fiction writers are less conservative, and, I will add, psychics are the least conservative. Since future technological events arrive *before* the less conservative estimates, we should disregard the more conservative dates. With that elegantly simple formula, let's look at some predictions I have culled from *The Book of Predictions*. I was a contributor to each one. When the predictor gave a time period, I took the earliest year. My "best bet" year is underlined. Compare with the average (Delphi technique).

Three-dimensional holographic television

Francie Steiger	psychic	1991
G. Harry Stine	scientist	2000
J. S. Maxmen	scientist	<u>1985</u>
Ian Miles	scientist	1990s
Alan Vaughan	psychic	1987
Average (Delphi technique)		1990.6

First solar-power satellite

Alan Vaughan	psychic	<u>1990</u>
Ben Bova	sci-fi writer	1993
L. S. Wolfe, R. L. Wysack	scientists	2000

Bertie Catchings	psychic	1992
Isaac Asimov	sci-fi writer	2000-
Average (Delphi technique)		1995

First manned flight to Mars

Arthur C. Clarke	sci-fi writer	2005
Gerald Feinberg	scientist	1992-
Bernard Lovell	scientist	1993-
L. S. Wolfe, R. L. Wysack	scientists	2010
Alan Vaughan	psychic	1992
Average (Delphi technique)		1998

Within eleven years we should be able to evaluate the Vaughan technique against the Delphi technique in projecting future technologies.

SCIENCE FICTION AS PREDICTION

Arthur C. Clarke's famous dictum on whom to believe about the future states: "When a distinguished but elderly scientist states that something is possible, he is almost certainly right. When he states that something is impossible, he is very probably wrong."

Here is my dictum on science-fiction writers: "When a distinguished science-fiction writer states personally that something is possible, he is almost always right. When his fiction says something is possible but he personally says it is impossible, his fiction should be given priority."

As a good example of a science-fiction writer making a statement of personal belief that should be disregarded, here are the opening words of Arthur C. Clarke's nonfiction book *Profiles of the Future*: "It is impossible to predict the future, and all attempts to do so in any detail appear ludicrous within a few years."

As exhibit one, I offer Clarke's 1953 masterpiece of science fiction, *Childhood's End*, which describes a future time in which children develop psychokinetic powers. In a disclaimer, Clarke disavowed any responsibility for this outrageous prediction: "The opinions expressed in this book are not those of the author."

In 1973, twenty years later, when Clarke was visiting London, he witnessed the Israeli psychic Uri Geller doing a psychokinetic demonstration. Geller's appearances on British television had galvanized thousands of children to copy his psychokinetic deeds—a few being accomplished under the watchful eyes of parapsychologists and physicists. According to an eyewitness friend at this demonstration, Geller appeared to dematerialize a part of a disc.

"My God!" exclaimed Clarke. "It's all coming true. This is what I wrote about in *Childhood's End*. I can't believe it!"

Another science-fiction writer who shares Clarke's nonfictional disbelief in prediction is Robert Silverberg. In a 1980 interview he said, "Science fiction does not predict—at least not in the usual sense. We look at patterns. We look for trends. We guess. It's hit and miss. When we aim for specific predictions, we miss enormously."

As exhibit two, I offer Robert Silverberg's 1975 novel, *The Stochastic Man*, which tells the story of a futurist scientist who develops his ability at precognition and combines the scientific and psychic aspects of prediction to achieve extraordinary accuracy. The stochastic man (stochastic means "pertaining to guesswork") sets up a think tank to refine guesswork into clairvoyant prophecy.

When I read the book in 1975 I was working at a think tank in northern California as a subject in psychokinesis experiments. My cosubject in these experiments was a futurist scientist who had developed extraordinary abilities in various types of psychic functioning, including precognition. He told me how psychic methods were being combined with scientific methods to predict the future. I wrote Silverberg that his novel was in fact predicting the future of prediction, and that its beginnings were at hand.

THE FUTURE OF PREDICTION

My real-life stochastic friend has asked to be anonymous, since, like the fictional stochastic man, he must conceal the source of his information lest it alarm his corporate and government clients.

Between bouts of disturbing a superconducting magnetometer, my stochastic friend told me how he and others at this think tank were synthesizing logic and ESP to come up with better answers. It turned out that many futurists were already using psychic techniques but did not realize it. They had not been tested for ESP—to them it was merely creative imagination about the future. But their techniques were nearly identical to those I use with students for psychic sensing of the future.

The method of combined logic and ESP (call it intuition if it is vague) first requires a collection of scientific data about a problem or trend in society. Alternate scenarios about the future are developed from this data. Then intuitive future visioning is applied to project what will happen if these alternate scenarios come true. The futurist may project himself to the year 2000 and look backward to sense the most significant changes and how they might have arisen. He looks forward in his intuitive mode to sense the outcome of a particular scenario. Several people working on a project do this, and the consensus of their future projections is considered the best guess about the future. Usually there emerge not one but several possible futures—depending on society's choices.

The next stage in the future of prediction will be the development of "surprise-sensing." Since so many traditional futurist scenarios fail because they depend on being surprise-free, futurists' psychic talents will be trained to look for surprises by pure psychic methods. This new development will save governments and corporations billions of dollars that are now currently wasted on programs that fail because the future was not correctly anticipated.

SURPRISES

Here I will predict some surprises that could save many billions of dollars if the government or industry should act on them now. (I doubt they will, but this is just to prove a point for the future.)

Surprise 1. The third space shuttle launch will have severe malfunctions that could threaten the space program.

Present action needed: NASA should have the shuttle craft thoroughly checked out by a team of psychics before the third launch to pinpoint the malfunctions, and prevent them.

Surprise 2. By 1984 the Russian KGB will have the capability of detecting which missile is in which silo in the MX missile program.

Present action needed: The multi-billion dollar MX missile program should be abandoned before it is built.

Surprise 3. By 1989 nuclear weapons will be outlawed and a firm arms reduction program will be in force.

Present action needed: Weapons and defense-related industries should inaugurate plans for alternate production of peacetime technologies.

Surprise 4. By 1989 efficient and fast battery-operated vehicles for city transport will outsell traditional gasoline-powered vehicles.

Present action needed: The auto industry can save billions by anticipating this trend and prepare designs for their own battery-powered cars lest the Japanese beat them to it.

Surprise 5. By 1985 the television viewing public will switch from viewing network programming to alternate programming by independent production companies.

Present action needed: The television networks should concentrate on providing sports and news coverage, and anticipate that their affiliates will be dropping most of their entertainment shows by 1984.

Surprise 6. In 1984 a citizens' tax revolt will become so strong that the U.S. government will have significantly less revenues than anticipated.

Present action needed: The government should inaugurate plans to allow taxpayers to specify which segment of service their tax money will go to, much as charities do. This direct involvement by citizens in government will cripple the arguments of the tax revolters.

Surprise 7. By 1989–1991 the demand for oil will plummet as alternate energy sources begin to supply more energy demands.

Present action needed: Oil companies should invest heavily in alternate energy development resources so they don't go broke when demand for oil goes down.

Surprise 8. By 1989 electronic publishing of books and magazines on specialized and technical topics will supplant scholarly and technical printing.

Present action needed: Specialized book and magazine publishers should invest in electronic technology for distribution of their products.

Surprise 9. By 1986 there will be a trend for shutting down large public school systems in favor of smaller, specialized schools run by independent educators.

Present action needed: The public school systems should anticipate smaller classes and inaugurate plans for their own specialized academies. Parents should anticipate planning with their children exactly what sort of education would fit each child's talents and ambitions. Millions of dollars will be saved as children and educators learn to serve each others' purposes better instead of perpetuating programs that bore them both.

Surprise 10. In 1989 American currency will be devalued by a factor of ten. New currency will be printed, with one new dollar being equal to ten old dollars.

Present action needed: None, since most of the world will follow the United States in readjusting its currency. The main impact will be psychological and practical. Just think: In 1989 you will be able to buy a house for less than $30,000!

FUTURE CHOICES

In the future the art of prophecy will merge with the science of prediction to achieve a reliability currently undreamed of. Beginning steps in this direction are being taken by the Mobius Group of Los Angeles, headed by Stephan Schwartz. By using teams of psychics to predict the outcome of specific events, such as the first flight of the space shuttle *Columbia*, and analyzing the data for consensus predictions to pinpoint future possibilities, the Mobius Group is developing a powerful technology of prediction.

Earlier, the Mobius Group demonstrated the practical application of psychic team consensus in archaeological projects—and discovered what may be the palace of Cleopatra, the palace of Anthony, and the lighthouse of Pharos in the harbor of Alexandria. A film and a book on that project are now in progress.

Mobius plans to link up by computer with the Central

Premonitions Registry in New York to carry out refined analyses of predictions and searches for talented precognitive sensitives. As a Mobius consultant, my own plans include a training program to develop and sharpen intuitive and/or psychic abilities for application in policymaking and societal choice making.

If more and more people learn to tap their psychic potential to see into the future, and learn how to rely on this skill in their everyday life, society will soon feel the pressure to employ futurists and psychics (stochastic men and women) to envision possible futures and show which societal choices will lead to which futures.

Once precognition has emerged from the world of the strange into the everyday world of business, government, education, and science, the stage will be set for a new leap forward: An enlightened society will have the wisdom to choose and fulfill its best future.

No matter how brilliant and talented psychics might become in predicting the marvels of the future, those marvels will not happen unless society acts to choose them.

We are treading on the edge of tomorrow with every choice we make. Once planted in the corridors of time, our footsteps can never be retraced.

EXERCISES

Looking Forward

1. Select some area of future development that interests you. It can be anything—technologies, entertainment, economics, for example. Review the subject and read what experts might predict. Probably you have read something recently that excites your interest and curiosity about the future.

2. Now relax and let all the logical information drain out

of your mind. You might take a walk, or try meditation, chanting, singing in the shower, or just listening to music. Close your eyes and focus your attention *out there*—as if time were palpably in front of you.

3. Shift your awareness to the future, visualizing it in your mind's eye as a series of waves in the ocean of time. Now introduce your target. Let the target float across the time waves until it stops. Estimate how far away in years it might be.

4. Now ask specific questions about your target. What advantages might come from this future development? How might it change people's way of life? How might it change your life?

5. In evaluating your answers, give more credence to those images that appeared in visual form and that seemed to be accompanied by a strong gut feeling or activation of the solar plexus.

6. If no specific year came, try reciting the dates of the years ahead and pay attention to your gut feeling for giving you the right answer.

7. If you know other people who share your interest in this future development, ask them to do the same experiment. But don't tell them beforehand what you saw.

8. Collect their predictions and examine them for any sort of consensus.

9. If your prediction and any consensus group prediction goes against what the experts think, register your prediction with the Mobius Group, 2525 Hyperion, Los Angeles, CA 90027.

CHAPTER 9

THE FLEXIBLE FUTURE

Can we change the future? When psychics prevision a future event that does not come to pass, is it because they are wrong? Or because they foresaw a possible future that was changed? When disaster is foreseen, can that disaster be prevented? Let's look at the evidence.

FOREORDAINED FATE

In the annals of psychical research there are a number of stories of people who had a premonition of some disaster or death but were unable to prevent it. Such a premonition came to Robert Morris, Sr., an American agent for a Liverpool shipping firm in the eighteenth century. His son, Robert Morris, Jr., a framer of the American Constitution, tells the story in his biography of his father. The night before the elder Morris was to meet the ship *Liverpool* at a port in Maryland, he dreamed that he received a mortal wound from a cannon salvo fired in his honor. Morris told the ship captain of his premonition and said he thought it would be best to skip that landing party. The captain dismissed his dream as superstition and convinced Morris to attend. Morris obtained the captain's promise that the salute would not be fired until he or the captain gave the signal. So the captain told the gunner not to fire until he raised his hand.

Morris and the captain went to meet the ship in a rowboat. A fly alighted on the captain's nose, causing him to raise his hand to brush it away. The gunner thought it was the signal and fired the cannons—directly into Morris. Wadding embedded itself in Morris's arm, causing an infection that led to his death a few days later. Robert Morris's foreknowledge of his death was insufficient to prevent it. But note that it was his own choice to be talked into attending the landing party. His fate was self-ordained.

PREVENTING DISASTER

In February 1981, a San Jose area woman, Mrs. Frances Vernier, awoke with a horrifying dream that one of the nursing homes she ran was going up in flames—helpless old people were being burned to death in their beds. The dream premonition woke Mrs. Vernier at two in the morning; she sat in her rocking chair until dawn worrying. Unable to bear it any longer, she drove to the Saratoga Place Convalescent Center in the early morning to check out the house. She was about to leave when she discovered a fire burning around gas pipes near the furnace in the rear of the building. She told a nurse to call the fire department and got the residents out of the house.

When I read of this account I telephoned San Jose County Fire Chief Victor Marino, who testified that it was true. "With her dream and her intuition, Mrs. Vernier prevented a major disaster. In just a few more minutes there would have been an explosion—and these people would have been killed," Chief Marino said. He added, "I never believed in ESP, but this proves there's something to it."

It also proves that it is possible to avert a tragedy by acting on foreknowledge of a possible future.

I, too, have such a story. In February 1975 I gave a lecture on premonitions to a class at St. Mary's College in the East Bay of San Francisco. The next day the class teacher, a friend, telephoned to warn me that one of the students had a premonition that I might be involved in an accident on April 19. She relayed the student's warning that I should avoid traveling on that date.

Well, as things turned out, I did find myself traveling that weekend. My wife drove me to Monterey to give a lecture. I told her about the premonition, and she was keeping an extra watchful eye on traffic. After the lecture, about two in the morning of April 19, as we were returning to our hotel after stopping at a nightclub, I said for no particular reason, "Let's make a left hand turn here."

Diane stopped to make the turn, even though we had a green light. At that instant a car speeded through the intersection—through a red light—at about fifty miles an hour. I breathed a sigh of relief and said, "That was our accident. We don't have to worry anymore." And so we spent the rest of April 19 without cause for alarm.

Apparently my inner self scanned the environment for the speeding car and gave me the impulse to suggest a turn.

Predicted events that *almost happen but do not* constitute the strongest evidence we have that the future is flexible—that it responds to human consciousness and choice. The flexible future necessarily limits the accuracy of precognition.

This theoretical argument came to a practical case in point on Easter Sunday in 1972, when I gave a lecture to science-fiction writers and fans at the New York City Lunacon. I described a premonition that a canister aboard the next flight to the moon, Apollo 16, would explode and cause the death of an astronaut. After the talk, a famous science-fiction writer approached me and made a remark that seemed to contradict his public skepticism about precognition: "You know, perhaps it would be worth the death of one astronaut to convince people of the reality of these things."

"I thought of that, too," I replied, reflecting that I had just told the group that I would make no more predictions of disaster unless something could be done to prevent it. I wrote Edgar Mitchell, a backup astronaut for Apollo 16, and detailed to him my premonition. I ended my letter with the words "Let us pray."

Apollo 16 went to the moon and back without mishap. But when a canister was taken back to the factory for examination, it exploded. Many people were injured. If the canister had exploded aboard the moon flight, it might well have killed an astronaut.

Was I foreseeing a possible disaster that was somehow averted? The question came into sharper focus in 1981, as preparations were being made for the space shuttle *Columbia*'s maiden test flight and landing.

PREVISIONS OF *COLUMBIA*

As the much-postponed space shuttle *Columbia* was being readied for its first flight, a television documentary showed the problems that had put it two years behind schedule. The most persistent problem was the more than 30,000 heat-shield tiles that had to be bonded one by one on the craft. If just one of them fell off the underside, the searing heat of reentry into the atmosphere—reaching 2,800 degrees—could lead to a disastrous fire.

After watching the documentary I did a psychic reading

on the future of the shuttle, and sent my January 6 prediction to the Central Premonitions Registry. (All the predictions quoted in this section were also registered with the CPR.) I foresaw a beautiful takeoff on April 12, though, as I have said, it was scheduled for March 17. On reentry I foresaw a tile (numbered 10935C) falling off the rear of the craft, leading to a rough landing and injury to the pilot on the left (John Young).

On January 22 I dreamed of the craft coming in too fast, swinging around and breaking the right wing.

On March 13 I had the opportunity to ask Beverly Jaegers about her impressions of the shuttle when we met in Atlanta on the child-killer case. Holding photos of the *Columbia*, she felt that something might fall off the rear of the craft. She foresaw a rough landing in which the right wing would break off. She was not certain her impressions applied to the first flight. But I was struck by the similarity in our impressions. Jaegers mentioned at the time her almost exact impressions might be coincident to being handed the material by me.

I convinced the Mobius Group that a psychic probe should be done on the *Columbia* with their team of psychics spread across the country and in Italy and Canada. Five respondents, including Jaegers and myself, foresaw danger. Another respondent described a computer malfunction very similar to the one that delayed the launch from April 10 to April 12. The Central Premonitions Registry received ten premonitions of disaster for the *Columbia*.

I was frantically worried about the *Columbia* and wrote Cable News Network in Atlanta on April 4 in the hope that I might be able to appear on *Freeman Reports* to alert NASA to present dangers so that they could postpone the April 10 launch to correct the defects. I knew from my experience with Apollo 16 that NASA's reaction to premonitions is to cross fingers.

At five in the afternoon on April 7 I received a strong impression that the space shuttle was saved. Somehow, in some mysterious way, our psychic data seemed to be acted upon. Now I foresaw the *Columbia* coming in for a beautiful landing. I wrote Cable News to cancel my request for an appearance. I felt jubilant that the space shuttle would work and inaugurate a new age of technology. I even conceived the notion that I would like a ride in it.

On April 9, at 1:09 P.M., I received the impression that the April 10 launch would be postponed. I notified *The New York Times*. A computer malfunction postponed the launch until April 12.

On takeoff some tiles fell from the rear of the craft. NASA engineers were so certain that tiles would *not* fall off that they had canceled orders for two tile-repair kits. Astronauts Young and Crippen brought the craft in for a beautiful landing—watched by millions on television.

I was so elated when the *Columbia* landed that I began to sing a song to my small children, "I Want to Make My Dreams Come True." My repeated visualizations of the *Columbia* coming in for a perfect landing, my dream, had come true. I bought the kids ice cream to celebrate.

Later I received a letter from Beverly Jaegers, written just before the landing, in which she told me that her final impression early in the morning of April 8 was that the craft would make a beautiful landing.

Somehow the crash landing we both had seen a month before was averted, and we both knew it as the time came near. Jaegers wondered if perhaps her impression on March 13 had come telepathically from me. That certainly is a possibility—indeed, one that I worried about at the time. But in view of the thirteen other premonitions of disaster, I tend to think we both were picking up the same possible future that was averted.

The big question is How? Perhaps there were millions of other people who also visualized and strongly hoped for a beautiful landing. Perhaps our collective consciousness changed the future. Somehow it was changed by 5:00 P.M. PDT on April 7, 1981.

Full details of all the premonitions and the experimental psychic predictions gathered by the Mobius Group would make a book in itself. And that would only be the merest beginning of a scientific study of the flexible future.

PROJECT CHICKEN LITTLE

The earthward plunge of *Skylab* in 1979 provided my first opportunity for investigating the flexible future—and a chance to cross prophetic swords with the National Aeronautics and Space Administration. Using the most sophisticated electronic and computer methods in the world, NASA was attempting to predict when *Skylab* would fall to earth. As to precisely *where* it would fall, a NASA scientist spokesman assessed their computer prediction capability with the statement: "There's no way in hell you can predict where it's going to fall."

To William Braud, a parapsychologist at Mind Science Foundation in San Antonio, Texas, the coming demise of *Skylab* at an unknown place and time provided an opportunity for a mass precognition test, which he called Project Chicken Little. I was one of 512 people who sent in their predictions of "the currently unknown impact location and impact time of *Skylab*." To get the location I psychically dowsed a small map Braud had sent to get a longitude and latitude; where the two lines met indicated my predicted target location: off the west coast of Africa, just above the equator. I also sent in a time prediction but later revised it because of a reaction that my wife and I had to NASA's prediction of "Chicken Little Day."

On May 30, 1979, when Diane and I were reading *Newsweek*'s report on Chicken Little Day, she objected that a better metaphor would be Icarus Day, since the sun was driving *Skylab* down four years too soon—much as the sun had melted Icarus's wings and plunged him into the sea. Our discussion of Icarus led us to a 1969 book of poetry in which the fall of Icarus was described on page 437, line 16. A strange, emotionally heightened feeling made us wonder if the book contained a code prophetic of *Skylab*'s fall.

North American Air Defense Command (NORAD), with its twenty-station tracking network, predicted that *Skylab* would start its final descent between June 20 and July 14—with Chicken Little Day being July 2. Yet our book of poetry, page 437, line 16, suggested July 16, with the possible hour as 4:30, and, as I guessed later, 4:37. I sent my revised prediction time to Project Chicken Little and waited to see if NASA and NORAD would revise their predictions.

A week later, on June 7, NORAD joined our book of poetry to predict July 16. An unexpected lull in radiation bursts from the sun was keeping *Skylab* up for two more weeks. On June 21, NASA radioed *Skylab* to turn sideways to increase atmospheric drag and, they hoped, avoid population centers. This changed NORAD's prediction for Chicken Little Day to July 12.

Also on June 21 I gave a press conference in San Francisco. The two major San Francisco papers, the Oakland paper, two television stations, and several radio stations carried my prediction: Chicken Little Day was to be July 16, with the two largest pieces of *Skylab* to land at 4:30 and 4:37 P.M. local Africa time off the west coast of Africa.

NASA and NORAD changed Chicken Little Day to July 11, but still did not know where and precisely when *Skylab* would come down.

On July 11, precisely at 4:37 P.M. local time off the west coast of Africa, *Skylab* lost radio contact as it broke up into pieces. It rained space junk over a 4,000-mile track across Australia. As soon as the breakup time was radioed across the nation, I received a telephone call from fellow precognition researcher Fred Blau, who had also entered the Chicken Little Day sweepstakes.

"My God!" exclaimed Fred, "You got the exact *minute!*" Blau had converted Pacific Daylight Time to local time off the west coast of Africa to realize the significant correspondence with my prediction of 4:37 P.M. The media, of course, did not, and anyway it was the wrong day. But for the record, the odds of guessing the minute and time zone of the breakup would be 34,560 to 1.

What does this tell us about the flexible future? NASA's decision on June 21 to turn *Skylab* changed Chicken Little Day from our mutual prediction of July 16 to July 11. NASA changed the future. Yet my 4:37 P.M. correspondence suggests there was a predetermined aspect to Chicken Little Day as well. Computers are unable to predict the outcome of such theoretically random events; human beings do better.

On the final scorecard of Project Chicken Little, not a single person of the 512 guessed correctly the impact location and time. But those predictions were registered before NASA started fooling around with *Skylab*. It seems to me quite likely that if the predictions had been gathered *after* June 21 there would have been a consensus prediction close to the Chicken Little Day time and place.

PERSONAL CHOICES

Our lives are full of choices. Sometimes we never know what could have happened if we had made a different choice. Sometimes we feel sure we made the right choice; at other times we feel just as sure we made the wrong choice. Just how much personal choice does the flexible future allow us?

Here is a parable of choice.

In 1972, while living in New York, I gave psychic readings for two friends, one an off-off Broadway actor and his friend, an off-off Broadway playwright. I told the actor that I saw a great future ahead of him as a star in Western movies. For the playwright I predicted a hit Broadway play.

Three months later the actor received a telegram from Western movie director Sam Peckinpah asking him to do a screen test for the lead of Peckinpah's next film, *Pat Garrett and Billy the Kid*. The actor panicked; he was, his friends said, fearful of success, or fearful of failing. He chose not to make the screen test. He did not fulfill the prediction. Kris Kristofferson played Billy the Kid.

Two years later, now living in San Francisco, I had the opportunity of seeing my prediction for the playwright brought to life on the stage. Robert Patrick's *Kennedy's Children* was such a hit on Broadway that it was taken on a national tour. I could boast that Patrick had fulfilled my prediction. But it is Patrick who gets the credit, not me. He recognized my prediction as one of his own guiding images and did his best to fulfill it. It was his choice and his creativity that led to fulfillment of his inner destiny.

FREE WILL VERSUS DESTINY

If we have an inner destiny—blueprint of life—how can we exercise our free will to make choices? For centuries the debate about free will versus destiny has misconstrued the whole matter of choice. We do not follow a destiny enforced upon us by some outside divinity; we are not puppets on a string. We follow an inner destiny *of our own choice*. Yes, we have blueprints—both biological and psychic—that limit us with our inborn potentials. But in the most important arena of choice—moral choice—our free will is supreme.

Many people speak of cause and effect. I prefer to speak of choice and consequence. Our inner destinies, like the rest of the universe, contain the seeds of the flexible future. When we choose which seed of our inner destiny to nourish, we plant the future consequences of our lives. Our lives do not just happen. They are created by our choices and the harvest we reap is our consequence.

We may choose to create challenges for ourselves so that we can learn. We may choose *against* the best blueprint of our inner self; the consequences will be disharmony and dissatisfaction with life. But sometimes, it is the worst of times that teach us the most—if we realize that it was our choice that gave us our present consequences. If we blame the universe or God or persons X, Y, and Z, we have not learned a thing—and probably will have to repeat the lesson.

Once we understand that it is we who are the masters of our universe—who make the choices that create the consequences of our lives—we become attuned to the very best that we can do and begin to fulfill our inner destiny. We influence the flexible future to go our way.

Often we make choices without much consideration of the future consequences. But if we learn to foresee the consequences of our choice, we learn to make better choices—how to foresee and fulfill our future.

LOOKING BACKWARD

From the vantage point of tomorrow, you can more clearly see the consequences of a present choice. The Looking Backward technique, also used by futurists, has several advantages over visiting psychics and counselors: It doesn't cost anything, it supplies the best answers (because they are yours), and you are more likely to act on your answers than on a stranger's advice.

When you are faced with a major choice in life, it is time to project yourself into the future and look back. A way to gain confidence in your ability to do this is to try it out with minor choices that give you feedback relatively soon: Will I like this movie? Will the boss like my new idea? Will my guests like a new recipe for dinner? What will happen if I decide to make a trip to Z?

To answer those questions, project your mind into the future just afterward and look back at the results. By paying attention to your feelings, you will quickly acquire the knack of intuitively choosing to do the right thing—both for yourself and others.

A related technique, which we shall explore in the Exercise section, is Attending Your Own Funeral. By journeying through time to attend your own funeral and listening to what people are saying about you, you may find out what is really important to you while you can still act on it.

These techniques fail when you try to project some strongly held fantasy from your ego self. In analyzing the imagery, you should review the criteria for sifting true images from false.

Bear in mind that our conscious minds—to maintain our sanity—must shut out details of events that we cannot now act upon. A strong assurance from our inner self that things will work out in the future because we have seen them, does not mean that we can now relax and let the future happen by itself.

The greatest lesson that the flexible future can teach us is that the future is created now. Our present choices and decisions select which possible future will become our reality. The future is created by our minds.

EXERCISES

Looking Backward

1. Think of a major choice in your life just now. What are the options? List two possibilities that appeal to you.

2. Let your mind travel five years into the future. In your mind's eye, look back over the intervening years and ask how things worked out with the first choice. Did it fulfill your expectations? Pay attention to your gut feeling about the final outcome. How was your life changed by your choice?

3. Repeat the same questions with the second choice.

4. Now compare your feelings and reactions to the outcomes of the two choices. Did one of them give a clearer picture and a better feeling? Did one of them seem dim and give you an anxious feeling?

5. Write down the choice that gave you the best feeling and seemed clearest. Now review it against the criteria of sifting false images from true in Chapter 6.

6. If your choice passed the test, consider how you might best be able to act on it.

7. If neither choice seemed really right, try projecting yourself once again into the future and ask, "How did I resolve the situation? What did I finally decide to do?"

8. Did you discover in your attempts at looking backward something that surprised you? You may have found a guiding image that you didn't know you had.

Attending Your Own Funeral

1. Let your consciousness travel to the distant future for your funeral. You do not know what year it is or what the cause of death is; you know merely that people are gathering together to talk about you and your contributions.

Friends and relatives are asking questions about you and making comments about how they judged your life.

2. In your mind's eye and ear eavesdrop on a conversation about you. You must be objective in your reaction to what they say. Your consciousness must merely record what is said so that you can react to it later.

3. Are they talking about what you accomplished in life? What were your most outstanding achievements?

4. Are they talking about the things you should have done but didn't? What was left undone?

5. Are they talking about how you helped and influenced others? How did your life enrich the lives of others?

6. Are they talking about your family? Did they have much to be grateful for? Were there things you should have done for them but didn't?

7. Now make notes of what you saw and heard. List them in two columns: a) Satisfying; b) Things to Be Done. Look over your list of things to be done and consider ways of doing them now.

8. Were there any surprises in the comments people made about you? If so, they might be guiding images that will assume importance in the future.

9. Did any of the comments made at your funeral suggest some action or choice that is pending right now? If so, did the experience give you any inspiration for present deeds?

CHAPTER 10

SHAPING YOUR FUTURE

How can we make our positive prophecies of life self-fulfilling? How do we make our dreams come true? Once we have found our dreams—our true guiding images of life—we must find the ways that work best to bring them into reality.

We are brought up to believe that honest toil, sweat of the brow, determined faith in oneself, courage, and perseverance will achieve our dreams. Those are all good ways, but the most important thing is lacking in that prescription for shaping our future: the mind. It is the mind that creates our dreams and the mind that shapes our future. If we master the understanding of the ways the mind works best, we begin to master the ways in which our dreams come true.

SCIENTIFIC RESEARCH

Most people don't realize that the subject of parapsychology is really the study of how the mind creates reality. The scientific research done by parapsychologists in investigating the creative powers of the mind is hardly known outside of a small group of people interested in psychic phenomena. Technical terminology creates a barrier to understanding for the average person, but the fundamental findings of psychic research apply to the daily activities of every living soul. These findings can teach us how to use our minds to influence and shape our present and future. They can teach us how to overcome disease, how to achieve goals, how to accomplish miracles.

Perhaps you already follow some teaching that promises this sort of understanding. There must be hundreds of philosophies and religions that all claim to have the answers to such questions of basic lifemanship. These different approaches to understanding have one thing in common: they are untested; we must take them on faith. It is the business of science to test claims and differing approaches. By repeated experiment the truth comes to light. In that way we can free ourselves from centuries of accumulated error through the transmission of philosophical and religious teachings.

The first question that parapsychology asked about the creative power of the mind was: Can the mind influence external reality? Calling this mind power *psychokinesis* and defining it as "the direct influence of mind on matter without any known intermediate physical energy," parapsychologists established that we can use our minds to change random events that are electronically generated by machines. Sixteen such experiments done between 1970 and 1975 yielded odds against chance of 10,000,000,000 to 1.

Psychokinesis (or PK for short) has been so well proven to exist, that now the main research efforts have shifted to finding out how to make it work better. What mental strategies work best in which situations? There was already an enormous popular literature that purported to give the answers. But, until the mid-1970s, no one ever thought to test them.

At the University of California at Santa Barbara, parapsychologist Dr. Robert Morris gave his students an assignment with far-reaching consequences. He asked them to read and digest as many books as they could find that purported to tell how best to use psychic powers. The class found seventy-four books by fifty-seven authors, mostly at the airport newsstands—hence the project's name: The Airport Project. The students found that two basic methods were advocated for shaping the future:

1. Process imaging—imagining in the mind's eye the details of the process leading up to the desired goal.
2. Goal imaging—imagining the goal in its final fulfillment without concern for how it happens.

The next undertaking of the Santa Barbara research team was to find out which technique worked better. Using college students and others of the same age, Morris and his colleagues did two studies to investigate the difference in these techniques when the students were trying to influence random event generators and getting feedback on their success. The *process* technique gave only chance results. And worse, the students who had no prior experience in mind training got below-chance results with process imagery. They were trying to imagine just how the machine might be affected by their thought but found that the machine did the opposite of what they wanted.

The *goal* technique, however, worked beautifully. The students racked up odds against chance of 10,000 to 1 when they imagined that they would get the desired result without worrying just how the machine worked. They foresaw the future in its final form—and it happened.

A similar study undertaken at Yale University by Ariel

Levi with fifty-one psychology students as subjects showed that the goal technique worked best when feedback was given. When the students didn't know how they were doing, the process technique worked better.

Not only did the Santa Barbara and Yale studies show the best ways to influence the future, they also showed that average college students are able to use their minds to affect external reality. PK, it now seems, is something that nearly anyone can do. Perhaps even every person can do it—or so I theorize—if the situation and the motivation are right.

I have years of experience in working with machines to demonstrate PK, and I can testify that it is far easier to work with human beings. The easiest situation in which to exert mind force is in affecting your own body. The greatest motivation comes when you are seriously ill, when medical science has given you up, and the only way to recover or prolong your life is to use your mind force to overcome physical disease.

Terminal cancer is the most dreaded disease we can have. "Terminal" means that doctors have already scheduled you for demise; medical treatment cannot prevent death nor, in many cases, even prolong life. It is such conditions that give rise to extraordinary motivations—for some. Others take their medical prophecy of doom to heart and fulfill it on schedule. Those who want to fight with all their powers can find a champion in Carl Simonton, M.D., and his wife, Stephanie, at their clinic in Fort Worth, Texas.

The Simontons advocate the use of mental power—process imaging—to accompany traditional cancer therapies. A stay at their clinic is expensive, but 240 highly motivated "incurable" cancer patients have come to try to lick the big C.

The Simontons ask their patients to visualize their immune systems as being very strong and destroying their cancer cells, which are to be seen as weak and disorganized. The patients choose their own visualizations—often like cartoon creatures seen on TV commercials. The good cells in white devour the bad cells in black.

The process style of imagery is used because the feedback to the patients takes a long time. But it does work. Of those 240 terminal patients treated between 1973 and 1980, the median survival rate is twice as high as those treated with conventional therapies only. And the really good news is that 10 percent of the patients have dramatic remission of their cancers.

Perhaps the greatest wonder of this work is that it is not available at *every* cancer clinic. The techniques are simple, the results a clear-cut improvement on traditional therapies, and there should be no lack of patients who would like to try to beat that death sentence. But apparently medical politics take precedence over the Hippocratic oath. As it seems to me, clinics will offer mind techniques only when patients demand it as their right in the pursuit of health.

An even greater success at treating cancer and other diseases with mind power will come when biofeedback techniques are utilized so that the goal strategy can be used. Patients will visualize themselves returning to perfect health, as being already well, and will receive signals from machines that measure their moment-to-moment progress. The greater effectiveness of goal strategy with feedback should dramatically increase the number of those who have remissions from terminal conditions.

LEARNING TO USE YOUR MIND

Our minds are used not only as computers for storing and retrieving information but also as creative tools for shaping our reality. It takes practice to get the mind working at its most effective level to realize our goals. It also takes feedback so that we know when we are doing something right. That is why the machines used in parapsychology are so useful: They are marvelous devices for training the mind to work little miracles.

Over the past ten years I have had the opportunity of working with many types of PK-measuring machines and devices, usually in laboratory experiments. In every case, I received feedback—the secret for strengthening mind power. I learned little by little just which strategy worked best with which machine. The more I learned, the easier it became. Part of that learning may, in fact, be merely the building of belief that one can do it. Once you have seen that your mind can affect a laser beam or a magnetometer or a random number generator, you believe it. It gives you confidence for the next impossible task.

Feedback is essential for the initial stages of learning, but once you have the hang of it, you can proceed without continual feedback. You can go ahead and create that future reality in the calm confidence that you know what you are doing. You *expect* your goal will be achieved because you have visualized it—you have seen it happen—and you know from experience that you are right.

So my translation of the Santa Barbara and Yale studies for use in everyday life is that feedback is needed for everyday initial success of goal-oriented imagery. But once you have learned that seeing is believing—that seeing your goal accomplished in your mind's eye is believing that it will happen—you have mastered the simple but effective technique of shaping your future.

I add a gimmick to that technique. It has not been tested in the laboratory but I find it works like a charm; so do my students. When I visualize the results of my goal, I see enthusiastic applause and cheering. Sometimes I even see that redoubtable character from the Muppets, Kermit the Frog, applauding with his unrestrained and heart-felt enthusiasm because I did so well. And who could doubt the sincerity of Kermit the Frog?

When I see and enjoy this tremendous applause and cheering in my mind's eye for something I have accomplished in the future, I ask myself: "What on earth did I do to provoke all that? It must be good. So I guess I should let myself do whatever it is that gets that kind of response."

When my future goal is applause, I find it helps me to get out of the way of my bumbling self, which worries a lot. I just assume that I'll get the inspiration when I need it; that I shall do the right thing at the right time; that others will respond in kind and that we'll all have a good time.

I have come to realize what should have been obvious to anyone. We exert the greatest PK effect on ourselves. When we project an outcome in our minds—when we see a goal fulfilled—we influence ourselves to fulfill it. And when we act to make the visualized goal a reality, we do indeed affect the external universe.

And there's an added benefit. Once we begin to use our creative mind force to make our dreams come true—to fulfill our inner destiny—the rest of the universe finds our dream irresistible. Others cooperate and help. They find in our dream a part of their own dream. We work with them and they work with us to make our dreams a reality.

The inanimate universe is also responsive to our mind powers. So-called things behave as if they have a consciousness; that consciousness wants to help, too.

We can become masters of our universe—not *the* universe, but *our* universe—in the same way that we are masters of our dream worlds, our bodies, our perceptions, our beliefs, our experience. The only universe we *can* know is our universe. So why shouldn't we be masters of all that we perceive and know?

The best way that we can learn to use our minds is to create an ideal universe that others will enjoy sharing. Our universe penetrates all the universes of all the people whose lives we touch. We share a dream. We share the ways in which we make our dreams come true. Our guiding images dovetail with their guiding images. Together we use our mind powers to shape a future that belongs to us all.

THE PATH OF FULFILLMENT

Religions often teach that the path of fulfillment is achieved by following the example of the religion's founder. Christians say, "Follow the example of Christ." But somehow Christ's message that everyone has the capability to do what he did is ignored. The following things he did should have set the example for being a good Christian: prophesy, heal the sick, materialize food for the hungry, advise fishermen where fish may be found (clairvoyance), identify those who would betray him (telepathy), forgive those who betrayed him (love), and materialize in a bodily form after death to show that he is eternal.

Christ said that it was "the Father within" who did the work, that each of us has a spark of divinity that accomplishes miracles, that belief would enable us to emulate him.

But strangely, modern Christians make no attempt to emulate the wonders of Christ, although they do attempt to incorporate love into their lives. What is worse, some groups of Christians teach that the wondrous miracles of "the Father within" are the work of the devil! Others who call themselves Christians even deny that we possess the abilities to "do the work." A strange condition indeed for a religion that is founded on what I might call psychic potential.

Some Eastern religions teach that psychic phenomena get in the way of the path of fulfillment—that true fulfillment comes only in a mystical union with God. In those traditions psychic abilities are mainly abused as sideshow attractions to impress the credulous with the godhood of the performer. It did not occur to ancient religious philosophers in those traditions that psychic abilities can be used to make a heaven, or Nirvana, on earth; they believed that Nirvana can be found only beyond the physical. So they paid scant attention to the now because the next existence beyond death is the only one with meaning. That slant can lead and has led to a great deal of present misery.

Attempting to strip away a few thousand years of misunderstanding, I find the core of most religious thought to be this: We are created in the image of God. We have a divinity, or creative consciousness, that partakes of the universe, that it is holographic and creates its own universe by means of its powers of mind. Created in the image of God, we are not only endowed with His powers but also His destiny: to create our own universes, to discover our inner destiny and fulfill it by prophesying and creating our future.

We do this not by listening to sermons or reading books but by discovering that it is we who have the keys to the kingdom, we who can unlock the mysteries of the mind to reveal our individual paths of fulfillment. Right here and now.

The fulfillment of our individual destinies does not happen as a solitary act. It can happen only in the context of human society. For society also has a destiny, and when we partake of that collective destiny we fulfill not only our own goals but those of the larger community. We help each other achieve a collective dream. True guiding images from our inner self stress the development of loving capabilities, healing and helping potentials, teaching and nurturing roles for the benefit of our young. The future of our dreams and the destiny of our collective civilization lie in the hands of our children. Thus our primary goal for self-fulfillment becomes the teaching of our children how best to fulfill their own lives.

We are poised on the brink of the next brave step in human evolution—a step that will take us closer to the day when every human being born into this world will have the opportunity to create his ideal universe. We adults are occasionally reminded that we use only a small portion of our mind and brain powers, but the scientists who tell us this never tell us how to increase our abilities, how to use that extraordinary reserve of mind force. We must learn for ourselves. One thing we should know for sure: If one person can do it, so can the rest of us. Once we see that the goal is possible, we can become like Olympic champions who set new records each year in perfecting the performance of the human instrument.

We who know of our potential path to a new evolutionary stage will act to fulfill it. Yet there will be many who prefer to complain that they don't know how, who think that young people should fend for themselves, who are satisfied with an absence of pain as their highest goal in life, and who are skeptical that the human condition can improve.

My advice to us who know better is to go ahead and do the best we can. Don't try to convert the skeptics; they will have to find out for themselves. If we set a few examples, if we show, through the abundant living of our lives, that we are indeed progressing toward this next step, it might occur to the others that they are missing out on something. They might just begin to get curious enough to suspend their disbelief. And once they open their minds, they might begin to join us. Our hope lies not in argument but in deeds.

SYNCHRONIZING WITH THE UNIVERSE

How do we know if we are truly following our inner destiny—truly realizing our guiding images? We may be visualizing some wonderful goal in the far future. How do we know if we are on the right track?

There is only one way to know for sure. When feedback

from the universe is positive, if your life becomes more satisfying to you and others, if your life works with a new ease and excitement, if barriers fall away, if opportunities open up, if life is a series of "yes" signs, you know your guiding images are being fulfilled. You are synchronizing yourself with the best opportunities both for your inner self and for the universe. Mostly, of course, this synchronization happens with others who share your dreams.

Here is a recent example of synchronization in my own life. I awoke one morning with a dream that symbolically told me not to continue putting effort into a foundation I had established. I had been able to get nonprofit status for it, but that turned out to mean getting about $20,000 in debt. Perhaps I should give the foundation to someone better qualified to carry out its goals of research? I asked one parapsychologist if she was interested. No, she had just investigated the legalities of such a situation and concluded it was not for her. My wife suggested that I call Jeffrey Mishlove, who had recently received his doctorate in parapsychology and had worked with me to establish a library for consciousness research.

As I reached for the telephone to call Mishlove in San Francisco, the telephone rang. It was Mishlove calling me—for the first time since I had moved to Los Angeles—to tell me that he and his wife were moving into a nice large house.

"Would you like a foundation to go with the house?" I asked. Of course he would. He would be able to maintain the library in this large house, which even had a special room in which seminars could be held. Our dreams seemed to be synchronized.

When feedback from the universe assumes a *negative* character, the message is: Rethink your goals and strategy. We learn more from our mistakes than from our successes, so pay attention to those "no" signs. They may, in fact, even be generated by your inner self to influence your environment to tell you that you are doing the wrong thing. Or that you may have the right plan but the wrong opportunity.

The latter seemed to be evident when I recently experienced a remarkable series of dissynchronizations, or "no" signs. I had moved to Los Angeles from San Francisco because of a series of dreams that told me I must get involved in the media. The dreams even spelled out my area code of 213 for Los Angeles. Everything went smoothly in the move and I found just the right house in two days, so that part of my life change seemed synchronized with my inner self.

My first opportunities for television appearances came soon after. Two producers from two new television shows somehow heard of me and asked me to appear on their shows. I visited one producer and talked with the other and hoped that we would be able to work something out. After all, I had come to Los Angeles specifically for such opportunities.

But my universe seemed to disagree: In the same day, two of my tooth caps broke off while I was vigorously flossing, two supports in my favorite chair broke and I had to throw it out, and twice a cabinet on the wall came crashing down. I just couldn't help noticing the coincidence of those "no" signs. I did not pursue the shows any further. When I finally saw them, I was grateful I had no connection with them. Both shows were terrible, I thought, and both have been canceled.

SOCIETY'S GUIDING IMAGES

To discover's society's collective dreams—the guiding images that we share—we must become the prophets of a new order. We must use our creative consciousness to become the science-fiction writers of reality. It might help to find out how science-fiction writers create their best worlds. Here is a tip from science-fiction editor and writer Ben Bova, who is executive editor of *Omni* magazine:

> To show other worlds, to describe possible future societies and the problems lurking ahead, is not enough. The writer of science fiction *must show how these worlds and these futures affect human beings.* And something much more important: *He must show how human beings can and do literally create these future worlds.* For our future is largely in our hands. It doesn't come blindly rolling out of the heavens; it is the joint product of the actions of billions of human beings. This is a point that's easily forgotten in the rush of headlines and the hectic badgering of everyday life. But it's a point that science fiction makes constantly: The future belongs to us—whatever it is. We make it; our actions shape tomorrow. We have the brains and guts to build paradise (or at least try). Tragedy is when we fail, and the greatest crime of all is when we fail even to try.

The prophetic visions of science fiction are seldom of paradise. As our society's visionaries, science-fiction writers and filmmakers often offer us negative images of tomorrow. They do this in the manner of a chiding parent who warns his or her offspring that the worst will happen if he continues acting the way he does. But just as sure as you tell a child never to stuff a bean up his nose, that child will stuff a bean up his nose. Negative warnings, prophesies of doom, scary tales of a future society gone mad, of scientific catastrophe and human debasement achieve the opposite of what their prophets hoped for.

Our consciousness is far more impressionable than most people realize. Studies of the effects of heavy media publicity on murder-suicides show a significant rise in accidental deaths on the highways and among pilots of small planes. Once implanted in our minds, negative suggestions can take over without our realizing it. Violence is a virulent disease that spreads from consciousness to consciousness. Negative expectations, pessimism, fear, and terror likewise spread like a contagion that infects a whole society. Negative visions characterize the expectations of our age.

Prophets of doom sell millions of copies of their books and cassettes. They have millions of followers who expect the worse, and in a perverse way look forward to Armageddon. This attitude stops progress in its tracks. As one observer put it, "You don't polish brass on a sinking ship." Why bother trying to improve things if it's all going to blow up anyway? Others head for the hills and stock up on provisions—and guns to keep away the city folk when Armageddon comes.

Yet there *are* visionaries of a positive future for us. Their books don't sell millions, their ideas are sometimes far-fetched or so they seem to mainstream folks, their writings appear in small publications like *The Futurist*, they have societies, like the World Future Society, they have meetings, they disseminate ideas about the future, they try to create a better future. Their day is coming soon.

Veteran future watcher Roy Amara, president of the Institute for the Future, in Menlo Park, California, characterizes those who best generate positive guiding images of the future as "visionaries, mavericks, or even geniuses. Such individuals possess a keen ability to view the world in unconventional and innovative ways that stimulate, educate, and stretch the mind. They tend to be intuitive and feeling in their thought processes and are effective writers who can communicate with mass audiences."

Think of visionaries of the past: Thomas Edison, a maverick genius without formal schooling who prophesied light; Dale Carnegie, who prophesied how to win friends and influence people; Bishop Fulton J. Sheen, who prophesied peace of soul to millions on television; and Norman Vincent Peale, who still prophesies the power of positive thinking.

In the 1980s and 1990s there will arise a whole new generation of visionaries who will find an audience for their positive visions of a society that works for everyone. The "me" generation of the 1970s will yield to a "we" generation of the 1980s. Replacing the cult of the self as center will be new philosophies embracing the society as opportunity for all.

If our collective vision of the future should be guided by our collective inner selves, we may discover that the diverse segments of our society agree on more things than they disagree on. I foresee a time coming soon when the dominant social attitude will shift from "I want my share" to "Let me share with you, so that you can share with me." We will become intently aware of being in this—this being the future—together. As our government's social programs are dropped (which I predicted in 1979), communities will band together to help their people in ways that will prove much better for us than the old method of government handouts. A new sense of community sharing and closeness will develop.

The 1980s will see the beginnings of a new style of social consciousness in which we will overcome our greatest problems by giving our young people the opportunity to fulfill their potentials. The old-style thinking, exemplified by fighting crime by building more prisons and employing more police, will give way to a more enlightened thinking that will help would-be criminals find meaning in their lives through their own creativity.

We are, at present, an imbalanced society in treacherous waters. Most of our attempts to right the balance are, as one wag said, "like rearranging the deck chairs on the *Titanic*." We are not getting to the core of our problems because society does not yet realize that only through future vision can we achieve that balance. We must all become visionaries to foresee that the best guiding images of society are those that, in the long run, give us *all* a chance.

We must ask of our society the same questions we ask of ourselves: What if I foresee how I can make things work better? Will I take steps to make it that way?

As a visionary friend of mine says, "Getting the vision is easy. It's making it come true that's the hard part."

Let us take Ben Bova's advice on creating the future and "show how human beings can and do literally create these future worlds." If we can see that future, we can believe it. Let us find those who share our vision and work to make our dreams come true.

EXERCISES

See the Goal

1. Before you go to bed at night, think about the things you have to do tomorrow. If some particular task or challenge comes to mind, see yourself in your mind's eye already having accomplished it. You see and hear applause from others because you did so well. They are cheering you. You take a bow. You are relaxed and confident because you knew all along you could do it well. Linger on the feeling of satisfaction.

2. The next day, after you have accomplished your goal, compare your actual feelings with those you experienced in your prevision. If you feel satisfaction, you have learned how to see the goal.

3. Repeat this regularly for about a minute each night before you go to bed or before some challenging task.

4. If feedback from your universe is positive, you are learning how to shape your future. If feedback is negative,

you may be trying too hard. Relax and don't push; just let it happen.

Fulfilling a Guiding Image

1. Select from your list of guiding images one that could be put into action now. It could be anything from communicating better with your spouse to writing a magazine article.

2. Now relax and see in your mind's eye an image of the results of your fulfilling that goal. Think of the last time you were successful at a similar task and recreate that feeling of satisfaction. Let the image and feeling of satisfaction stay in your consciousness for about a minute. See yourself being applauded for doing so well. You know it will be easy because you have seen it happen. Your spouse is happy at the attention you are giving your family and is returning your communication; your magazine editor is delighted to see your manuscript and is writing you a check.

3. If any ideas for action came while you were visualizing your guiding image, use it as a first step toward making your goal happen. Think of something interesting to tell your spouse; take a piece of paper and put on it a title for your magazine article.

4. Every day for the next few days, visualize your goal for one minute and feel confident that it will happen. Follow your spontaneous impulses. You might suggest to your spouse an evening on the town; you might write a lead for your magazine article.

5. Ask yourself if there is anything standing in the way of your goal that you can remove by your actions. You might give your spouse a book to read that you enjoyed so you will have something to discuss; you might do more research for your article to become an authority on the subject.

6. When the time seems right, complete your goal and get feedback on your success. You might spend a whole

evening talking with your spouse about your relationship; you might complete your article and send it to the editor.

7. Afterward, compare your initial visualization with what actually happened. Did your spouse confide in you? Did your editor like your article and send you a check?

8. If the goal was not achieved, try again. Make a greater effort to communicate with your spouse; write a new magazine article and send the first one to another magazine editor.

9. Keep up your visualizations for as long as it takes to accomplish your goal. If the goal is a true guiding image, it will be fulfilled—sooner than you may think.

CHAPTER 11

TIME WILL TELL

Time, like space, has always seemed to most people like such a constant thing. Clocks, chronometers, celestial timekeepers like the sun and the moon, with their regularity, make us aware of an eternal rhythm. We set our electronic watches to the second, we synchronize our lives to time, and it all seems to work.

We become aware of different kinds of time. A moment in a dentist's chair stretches out to seem longer than an entire night spent in a lover's embrace. That's psychological time, we tell ourselves; the differences are only an illusion.

When Albert Einstein introduced the concept of relative time and space, he shocked the scientific community. Experiment showed that time is distorted by speed and mass, and we comforted ourselves with the notion that that sort of thing doesn't happen here on earth. It only happens out there, in the vast reaches of the heavens, and perhaps in those mysterious theoretical entities known as black holes. A black hole, we are chilled to learn, is so massive that it squeezes the space and time out of matter.

The beginning of the universe is just as bothersome for our concepts of space and time. Astronomers have tracked the radiation from the initial Big Bang that created space, time, and matter in an instant. We cannot speak of *before* that instant because there was no time. We can speak only of the universe being born in a cosmic explosion about fifteen billion years ago. It comes as a surprise to most of us that space and time are still being created on the edges of the universe.

When I try to conceive of how this enormous universe of galaxies, nebulas, stars, planets came out of nothing, my head hurts. When I try to understand how time, space, and matter were instantaneously created, my headache worsens. My logical mind just cannot conceive of all this. So I have to turn the problem over to my intuitive mind, and see what happens.

Here is the picture I get: Almost like the biblical story of creation, a consciousness outside of space and time conceived of a universe and brought it into being in an instant. He (that cosmic consciousness) gave his own qualities to this new universe of space, time, and matter. It, like He, is holographic: The whole is contained in each of its parts; each part can reconstruct the whole.

The universe was born with a purpose, a destiny. What seem like random events in the enormity of time have, in reality, direction and purpose. For one thing, they enabled us—human beings—to be created in the image of the cosmic consciousness. We, like He, have individual destinies. We, too, have a purpose; we, too, create our own universes; we, too, create space, time, and matter.

In order to create time, we do not have to know a whit of theory. We need only consciousness, which selects which probability will come into reality. We influence random events to line up in the long run according to will. Our mind force not only influences reality, but, collectively, *creates* it.

Suppose that this is so. Does it give us any advantage in

living our lives? Can this knowledge, if it is true, enhance the ways in which we might fulfill our destinies?

Consider this idea. The way we experience time is the perception of a collection of events: The faster events are experienced, the more time seems speeded up; when events come slowly, our sense of time is slowed. If, for example, you are watching cars go by, and a hundred come and go in an hour, you experience a rapid passage of time. If only one car comes by, you sense a slow passage of time. The experience of time is relative to the number of events.

If we foresee a distant goal and focus our mind powers to achieve that goal, our success will depend on how many events we can influence. If you want to have a baby by next week, for example, all of your concentration will not help. If you want that baby within five years, you have a good chance, because there are thousands and thousands more random events that you can influence. And, of course, because it takes a gestation period for the baby.

If our consciousness foresees a future event, that very act of precognition makes the event more likely. When we touch things with our minds, we change them. Physicists speak of the "observer effect" to mean the same thing on the quantum level. I suggest it happens also in our daily lives. When we observe things in the future with our minds, we are helping to create them. We self-fulfill our prophecies.

So when you foresee a baby within five years, your very act of prevision influences you to make it happen. That shouldn't be too much of a surprise. We are always planning future events—seeing them in our minds—and then taking action to bring them about. The surprise may come when we consider that the further away our goal is in time, the better chance we will have to accomplish it.

The elevator experiment cited in Chapter 4 gives some evidence for this idea. The subject got his highest scoring rate (77 percent) when he was trying to predict over the greatest period of time (sixteen hours). I think his very act of prediction influenced the future arrival times of the elevator; the more events that could be influenced over time, the better his success.

But did you ever say, "I don't want to think about the future. I don't have time to cope with the present."

We all have said that at certain points in our lives, usually at desperate moments. Mostly, they came about because we had not thought about the future before them. Because we did not exercise our gift of foresight (or prevision) in the past, we pay in the present with a feeling of panic and inability to cope. We get caught up in the problems of the present and tend to exclude from our thoughts the very necessary prevision of the future that will lessen our problems later. The next time you get caught up in the feeling of not wanting to know the future, consider that by wanting to know, you can actually improve the future. The future is not something that happens by itself.

I have already suggested that we create time. Now I suggest that we create the future. If you think about it, those statements are really identical. The future consists of time units, of a measuring of events, and the events in turn are selected by our consciousness. But since each of us experiences his or her personal universe a little differently, each of us creates time a little differently. We express our individual personalities in the creation of time and the future.

That statement may seem shocking to those who regard time as a constant. But the evidence is compelling. Although the greater universal consciousness (as far as we can surmise) *collectively* creates a framework of time and space, we, as individuals, create our *individual* universes of time and space. We foresee events in different ways; express our individuality through precognition.

We can foresee events both in our lives and in the lives of others. There is, however, a difference between the two experiences. When we prevision events in our own lives, we tend to make them happen; we are the primary psychic observers who influence those events. When we foresee events in someone else's life, we are, like viewers of a movie, not responsible for their creation; we are secondary observers. It may be quite true that we exert *some* small influence, but it is miniscule compared to that of the author of the life events we foresee. It is a difference that assumes importance when we think about premonitions. If I foresee the crash of an airplane or an assassination, I am no more responsible than a moviegoer watching such an event on the screen. But if I foresee an event in my own life, I am involved: It is my movie and I have the final cut. The responsibility is mine.

What happens when many people foresee the same event? If the event is a large-scale happening that could affect the lives of all in the group, the future event will tend to happen. If millions upon millions of people foresee the same outcome—such as the perfect landing of the space shuttle *Columbia*—it helps that future to happen. The influence of television may be paramount in influencing public events. If people are not only alerted to a possible future but are given actual images of it to help their own efforts at prevision, it becomes easier for them to see it happen. The future of space flight involves them all. The advent of space technologies becomes a global phenomenon that affects the future of the whole human race, so everyone assumes some responsibility for that future.

If that is true, so are the negative possibilities. If many millions of television viewers are alerted to the possibility of an Armageddon, and are given images of that terrible future to help them prevision it, it will tend to happen. War is a powerful archetype of the collective consciousness; it needs only a minimum amount of psychic prevision to activate it, and once activated it tends toward completion.

Societal futures, both positive and negative, seem to be out of our individual control. Each of us contributes to those futures, yes, but in such a small proportion that it becomes frustrating to attempt any influence over such massive events. The best thing to do is to concentrate our previsionary abilities and our life's energy to select our own best possible futures with the knowledge that if we live our lives abundantly we shall contribute to an abundant society.

If we as individuals experience success in foreseeing and fulfilling our best futures, we gain confidence that the same techniques can be used in our communities. Once we understand how to make our own lives work better, we will be better prepared to make society work better. Once we have the experience, we can work together to achieve a mutual resonance of vision and the will to accomplish our collective goals.

It is my belief that we can achieve our utopias *only* by developing our individual talents for creating a better future. We do not fulfill our collective destinies by accident, but rather by applying our godlike powers of mind. We shape tomorrow from the fabric of our inner destinies with the tools of our creative consciousness.

IS IT TRUE?

Is there any way of testing what I have said? Can scientific experiment determine if my theory is true or if it is just one of hundreds of untestable theories proposed over the millenia? Many modern theorists of precognition and psychic phenomena have offered explanations, models, insights, have described psychic processes, and have made many contributions to understanding psychic functioning at several levels. But they have not proposed a testable theory. They have not yet offered a theory comparable to Einstein's simple but fundamental equation of $e = mc^2$.

Well, I don't claim to have outdone Einstein, but I do have a testable theory. It may be right; it may be wrong. But at least scientific experiment can find the truth. And if it is true, it might have far-reaching possibilities of application. Recall that Einstein's simple equation of $e = mc^2$ made possible the development of atomic energy.

My basic statement of reality is not an equation, but has to do with relationships of relativity. Time is relative to human consciousness; space is relative to human consciousness; matter is relative to human consciousness. The success of human consciousness in creating space, time, and matter is relative to the available number of events it can foresee and influence.

I have proposed a dozen experimental tests of this theory. The basic idea for these laboratory tests is that space, time, and matter will vary according to psychological variables of the subjects in psychic testing; and that the results should not be affected by preexisting parameters of space, time, and matter.

In matters of prevision and providing we will be given feedback for an event in our future, the theory predicts that our success at seeing through time will tend to improve with the greater number of events that will contribute to the final outcome; and that, conversely, so-called time constants will not affect our success. If, for example, I try to predict the color of the one thousandth car that will drive by, my success will not be dependent on whether that happens in a week, a month, or a year—so long as I am there to see the car drive by and know it's the target car. If the cars come by at a constant rate, my chances for success will actually improve with time; my prediction, say, of a brown car to be the one thousandth may actually influence the driver of a brown car to fulfill my prediction. The more cars available for influencing, the better my chances of success.

In the laboratory it would be electronic devices that generate the targets. And because electronic events happen by the billions, they are more easily foreseen and influenced: When we observe them in the future, we, by that very action, tend to influence them.

The aspect of the theory that has the greatest potential for application resides in the holographic (or holonomic) nature of consciousness. Each of us possesses a fragmentary piece of the collective consciousness of the universe. So we potentially have access to all knowledge of the universe, albeit in fuzzy and fragmentary form. The Mobius Group, headed by Stephan Schwartz in Los Angeles, has already demonstrated that individual respondents to psychic questions answer imperfectly, but that when their statements are examined for consensus, a more accurate and dependable answer emerges.

This technique can be improved upon, I believe, when individual psychics are brought together in groups so that their consciousness can unite into a collective field. The more pieces of a holographic structure that are joined together, the greater the definition and clarity of their collective vision. The techniques needed to achieve this collective psychic vision will not be difficult to develop. Several experiments have successfully used groups united in their consciousness to achieve a collective result far more accurate than that of any one individual. More experimentation along these lines is planned.

Time will tell if my theory and its possible applications will lead to the development of holographic consciousness technology. If I do my job as prophet well, and many others begin to envision a future enhanced by consciousness technology, we stand a better chance for making that dream come true. To improve my odds for success, I shall devote the last chapter to prophesies of fulfillment through consciousness technology. I'm betting that many of you will recognize some of your own guiding images in my future vision of the third millennium's beginning.

HUMAN DESTINY

Where is the human race going and how will we get there? Do we have within our collective psyches blueprints of our ultimate destiny?

Those are questions modern-day science cannot answer. Most scientists do not even think the questions have any meaning. They think we are just a fortunate accident that happened by a series of longshots throughout the enormity of time. And so any future for us would also be a series of accidents, for materialistic science has no concept of consciousness creating its own reality.

Yet there are, I believe, scientific principles at work in forming our destiny. And it is even part of our destiny to discover those principles and utilize them to hasten our voyage through time and space. When we become historians of our past, we see the roots of our future. Human beings have an urge to explore, colonize, and explore some more. We are always seeking new frontiers to conquer and make in our image.

Our psychic heritage from millions of years ago will not quietly disappear now that opportunities for terrestrial exploration and colonization have petered out. The urge is too strong. We are like salmon that must seek their breeding place to spawn a new generation. We will not rest until we plant our seed in the stars, for it is *out there* that the universe began, it is out there that *we* began, along with all the rest of creation, and it is our destiny to find our home in the stars.

How will we do this? Our scientists tell us that the speed of light is the absolute speed limit of the universe. The vast reaches of the stars are so far by our terrestrial standards that we cannot even comprehend that kind of distance.

But if I am right in saying that we create time and space, the problem of traversing great spans of time and space changes to the problem of how to create space-time so that we can be where we desire. We do not traverse anything— we are just suddenly there. To master that ultimate technique of space-time teleportation, we must first master our own consciousness. And this will necessarily entail our working together on a profound level of meshed consciousness that can achieve results undreamed of for an individual.

If this sounds like science fiction, it may be because science-fiction writers are tapping the same collective dream of humankind's destiny. If it seems impossible today, that is only because we have not yet seen it so that we can believe it.

Let's consider the earlier stages of human evolution that might lead to such an extraordinary development that now seems so impossible. To do so, we must have an insight into the nature of human evolution. Human beings are the quintessence of computer capability. Our exquisite circuitry is programmed with a highly complex series of instructions. We can see this most clearly in the development of a fetus and in early childhood, when changes come so quickly. Each programmed stage must be reached before the next circuit goes into operation. We speak of developmental stages. But potential circuits of the brain are there, waiting for the right signal to put them into operation. This development process does not stop when adulthood is reached; it only slows. Whether or not additional circuits are triggered into operation depends not so much on the signals from the glands but on the mental preparation of the adult. If an individual pushes his or her capabilities to their extreme, he or she automatically triggers the next circuit's operation.

That is a computerese way of saying that we possess potentials for genius that can be achieved only by trying. And the type of genius I'm talking about is achieving mastery over space, time, and matter as well as the more conventional notion of being a brilliant thinker and problem solver.

If we are created in the image of God or the cosmic consciousness, the evidence is that God must be the ultimate computer—going far beyond our limited concepts of what a computer can do. As further evidence, we have the urge to create beings in our own image—and create computers. They are getting better all the time. When we imbue them with human personality, we call them robots. Our filmmaker visionaries have given us Hal (in *2001: A Space Odyssey*), R2D2 and C3PO (in *Star Wars*), and endless numbers of spinoffs both malevolent and cute, in other movies and TV productions. Our scientists are not far behind.

The movie robot-computers capture our imagination because they satisfy our urge to create beings in our own image. When those fantasies become a reality, you can be sure that our robots of the future will indeed have personalities.

The future development of robotics will be tied in with our own development. As we open up new circuitry, we will pass on to them the latest capabilities we have discovered. We may even succeed in imbuing our future robots with an intelligence that surpasses that of anyone living today. Those future robots will help us build new technologies that will be linked with our own minds to achieve extraordinary control over space, time, and matter.

Once we achieve that control, we shall be on our destined ways to the stars in search of our maker. What we shall find may surpass the fantasies of science fiction. Arthur C. Clarke, in *Childhood's End*, speaks of our destiny to join the Overmind. Clarke is only spinning a tale of fantasy, he says. But many other tales of fantasy have come true. This one, I believe, will happen before the dawn of the fourth millennium on January 1, 3001.

Time will tell.

EXERCISES

Guiding Images of Society

1. Select from your guiding images one that could benefit society as a whole.

2. In your's mind's eye, imagine how that guiding image might be accomplished. Would it take cooperation from other people?

3. Ask some friends to your house for a goal party. Tell them that they will have a chance to express their hopes for the future and for society. Tell the group of your goal for yourself and for society. Then ask each person to tell what their goal might be.

4. If there are any similarities or dovetailing of goals, encourage discussion between people who share the same vision. You may find someone who shares your dream.

5. Ask the group if anyone has been able to achieve a similar goal in the past. How did he or she do it? You may get some good ideas.

6. If you or others find you share some goals, arrange to get together more frequently to discuss ways of helping each other accomplish the goal. It would be best if the whole group can agree on a single goal.

7. Think about your goal every day and visualize it being fulfilled for about a minute. In your visualization you may sense some inspiration of how to accomplish it.

8. When you meet again with the others who share your goal, mention any ideas or inspirations you may have. See if the others have any new ideas. Talk about them.

9. If your sharing of information with others has produced some plan of action to accomplish your goal, consider that the plan could start with you.

10. If there is some small thing that could be done to get a little closer to your goal for yourself and society, find a way to begin. You may find that you can begin with the help of the others.

11. After you take the first step, you may find that you have ideas for further steps.

12. Take one step at a time.

CHAPTER 12

2001: A PROPHETIC ODYSSEY

On the forefront of the future—the edge of tomorrow—lies the most powerful technology ever devised: the technology of human consciousness. Once we accept responsibility for our future realities and achieve a profound belief in our godlike powers of mind, the sky is not the limit—it is only the beginning.

The next twenty years may be the most crucial era in our history. In that crucible of challenges will be forged not only a new will to make the future work but the beginnings of a new era of human evolution. It will not be easy. Prophets of doom sap our will and darken our vision of the future. The precipice of disaster seems to loom ever closer with each new report of war and rumor of war. Much of the world is fearful. Staring into the faces of the horsemen of the Apocalypse, some are hypnotized with terror and surrender hope.

Perhaps we have reached the bottom of Pandora's box. After the evil forces have been unleashed in our world, when we are despairing, we find hope.

Join me in a prophetic odyssey to the advent of the third millennium. It begins on January 1, 2001. As we celebrate the new year, the new century, the new millennium, will we also celebrate the condition of the human race? Time will tell. And it will tell the most to those who have foreseen it. Listen to your own intuitions, your own hearts, and judge if my prophecies of the dawning of an era of consciousness technology will become a dream of promise for our collective future. It can happen only if you believe it can. It can happen only if you, too, foresee it. It can happen only if you share that dream and act to make it come true.

PROLOGUE

When the Russians unveil their psychic weapons development program in 1984, the world is shocked. U.S. government officials did not believe it was possible, but now the U.S. military is demanding massive funding for defense projects to counter the new weapons. The MX missile system has to be scrapped. Soviet psychic detection made it obsolete.

Military funding of psychic development projects extends to the universities and private laboratories. By 1989 new developments in refining psychic and consciousness techniques are developed by think tanks, and are widely adopted in government and industry. These techniques spread to education in high schools and colleges. Students develop their talents for using intuitive, psychic means for application in many areas.

In the so-called ESP war between the United States and Russia, the United States is found to be the winner—by default, since the Soviet attempts to wield psychic abilities to harm others backfired on them. Many of the Russian "black magicians" become insane, unable to cope with the fear of psychic retribution from others. In this way it is learned that consciousness technology cannot be used for aggression, only defense. Would-be Darth Vaders quickly learn not to fool with "the Force."

After the war, the American programs in consciousness technology are kept because they have already proved their usefulness. These programs begin to be felt in every sector of society.

EDUCATION

By 1991 high-school and college students are being taught how to balance their left and right brain functions with biofeedback devices. Students are learning to use their intuition and ESP in problem solving along with logic to find the answers that work best. Enhanced brain functioning combined with advanced techniques in learning enable students to memorize in an hour what formerly took a week. Emphasis on learning shifts to creative thinking and learning how to learn. Renewed interest in the creative arts accompanies this new approach. The performing arts, writing, music, art, dance and other esthetic pursuits find a strong place in the curriculum.

Vocational counselors for young people now use psychic and consciousness techniques to help students make the right career choices. Vocational training begins in high school, especially for students whose talents lie in practical areas. Under the supervision of retired experts in many career areas, young people who formerly dropped out now receive pay for training and working in special apprenticeship programs financed by local communities.

Many students are opening up their own small businesses and learning how to be productive. Financing for these businesses comes from local communities, which also supply retired businessmen as advisers to keep the students on track. The retirees derive great satisfaction from their productive work, and some become senior partners with the young businessmen.

Special programs are enacted for the academically gifted so that these students can develop to the height of their potentials. Their innovative contributions to society have already made the program pay for itself.

CRIME

Due to the burgeoning opportunities now open to young people, there are fewer school dropouts and bitter youths trying to get back at society by committing crime. By 1995 urban street gangs have vanished. Youths are finding productive and satisfying work in small business and shops financed by community loans. Fewer police are needed in urban areas.

Police recruits are routinely tested for psychic ability. Those who show unusual talent are trained to use their abilities to increase the efficiency of crime detection and enforcement. Criminals are quickly apprehended with these psychic techniques. When hardened criminals learn how easily they can be caught, many of them decide to try some safer occupation.

Criminals who are sent to prison receive intensive rehabilitation through consciousness techniques that help them realize that they can make their lives what they want them to be. Parole officers have helped paroled prisoners find satisfying careers in special programs financed by the states. Many parolees are paid to learn new vocations, and those who want to start their own businesses are lent state funds. Criminal recidivism dramatically drops, and states find that they are spending far less money in their new programs than they spent on housing prisoners.

During their prison stays, criminals have opportunities to develop their psychic talents; they become aware that if they harm others, they are harming themselves. After release some ex-convicts become leaders in their communities, some work with the police in inspiring young offenders to leave lives of crime for productive and satisfying work in the community.

ENERGY

By 1989 oil companies are regularly using psychic and consciousness techniques to improve their chances of success in the exploration and drilling of new wells. Where formerly they found oil only 10 percent of the time, now 60 percent is considered acceptable. This 500 percent increase in efficiency has lowered the price of gas and oil, and provided new funds for research into alternative energies and better use of conventional fuels.

By 1991, as the new energy research programs begin to pay off, the oil demand lessens, and oil companies change their names to energy companies as their new investments in alternative energies bring greater income than oil.

When consciousness techniques are applied to the development of nuclear fusion power plants, nuclear fusion becomes a cheap, reliable, and safe method of producing electricity. The old atomic power plants are replaced by fusion plants to meet increased energy needs. The first fusion plant with this new design goes into operation in 1993.

THE ARMS RACE

By 1989, when the Russians and the Americans realize that both have refined psychic techniques for accurately detecting where atomic missiles are located and that they both have the capability of detecting atomic explosions, they agree not to build any more nuclear warhead missiles.

When an atomic device is exploded in the Middle East, the United States and the Soviet Union are spurred to disarm all nuclear weapons and establish an international nuclear arms regulatory commission to ban nuclear weapons in all countries. Equipped with a few nuclear missiles to enforce the ban, the United Nations Nuclear Arms Regulatory Commission uses psychic techniques to insure that no secret bombs are built by any country.

By 1991, now that world tension is lessened, the United States and the Soviet Union agree to reduce their military budgets by 5 percent each year. Half of the money saved goes to the United Nations, half to the economies of their own countries. In the Soviet Union people who were trained to become psychics during the ESP war developed visionary qualities and are now demanding that their government's money be put to use in building a better society. The Soviets make swift progress under the tutelage of the ESP war veterans trained in consciousness techniques.

SCIENCE

In the late 1980s think tanks begin using consciousness techniques to speed up scientific progress. A team of scientists and psychics at a California think tank discover the principles of antigravity in 1988, and by 1992 the first manned flight to Mars is planned using antigravity propulsion systems. Since the new system does not need rockets, the astronauts can use a space shuttle that is already built; they equip it with the simple antigravity device and slowly take off. As they leave the atmosphere, their speed increases to a hundred times that of rocket ships. Their landing on Mars is as gentle as their takeoff, and their return trip is easier than that of the first space shuttle. They don't have to glide through the atmosphere; they float down.

Long-standing plans for a space station in orbit around

the earth are now activated. With the antigravity propulsion system it becomes easy, fast, and relatively cheap to transport material into space. Refined radio telescopes detect signals from extraterrestrials when guided to the proper coordinates by teams of psychics. The psychics help decode the transmission, and contact with other minds begins.

New breakthroughs in science and technology accelerate as think tanks become more skilled in the use of consciousness technology to solve long-standing problems.

MEDICINE

By 1989 medicine begins to make widespread use of biofeedback techniques coupled with consciousness techniques to treat progressive diseases such as cancer. As more people realize the role of their own consciousness in producing disease, doctors make use of consciousness techniques to help patients heal themselves without surgery or drugs.

The emphasis of medicine is now to prevent disease. Using psychic treatment techniques, doctors become skilled in treating their patients with what used to be called the "placebo effect." Regular counseling sessions with patients while they are well dramatically reduces the incidence of disease.

In 1991 medical schools introduce short (three-year) programs for lay doctors who are trained primarily in patient care and teaching patients how to heal themselves. Many nurses opt to become lay doctors, actively promoting healing by consciousness techniques and counseling preventative medicine. More than 80 percent of patients who paid for regular doctor care in the past now find that lay doctors are cheaper and more effective in dealing with their common ailments. Many minority people become lay doctors and start programs in ghetto areas, ushering in a revolution in health care for the poor.

The dramatic drop in hard-core patients needing expert medical care releases more M.D.s to do medical research, which is funded by the new health care plans that are now making money. The new preventative medicine techniques become so effective that the cost of medical care plummets.

Medical schools now have courses in psychic diagnosis, which speeds up the diagnostic process. Medical research teams utilize consciousness techniques to come up with improved treatment and breakthrough cures for formerly incurable diseases, such as muscular dystrophy.

The common cold becomes a thing of the past as more and more people adopt the self-preventative technique of ten minutes of self-healing each day to keep themselves healthy. Their improved immune system proves more resistant to common ailments.

GOVERNMENT

By the 1992 presidential election, pressure from citizens who have learned consciousness techniques exerts enough influence to put into party platforms the promise that the best futurist/psychic consultations will be sought before major programs are budgeted.

Many people still feel the old way may be best for government, but a growing number of voters want to see psychic probes done on the candidates to find out if they are telling the truth and will fulfill their promises.

A growing grass-roots community movement wants tax dollars to go directly to the local communities rather than to the federal government. A compromise is reached in which federal taxes are reduced by half, so that local communities can raise money through income taxes. The community income taxes are lower, however, and more money stays in the taxpayer's pockets. Federal government programs are slashed, and the local communities take over their functions. Taxes become lower as the effects of decreases in the military budget are felt.

Government at all levels becomes more efficient and less costly as consciousness techniques are routinely used to aid in making decisions and solving problems.

By the year 2001 the federal government has substantially reduced its budgetary needs—since so much tax money goes directly to the communities without going through federal bureaus—that it has decreased in size and its responsibility for domestic programs. More and more, the country is running itself.

The U.S. president is no longer regarded as a celebrity but more like the chairman of the board, who keeps a low profile and spends his time making decisions. Foreign policy now becomes the president's chief responsibility. His work is made easier by teams of psychics and consciousness researchers who monitor foreign developments with such accuracy that foreign countries now realize they can no longer keep secrets from us, and we realize that soon we will not be able to keep secrets from them.

THE ECONOMY

By 1994 the national economy has improved in many areas by the widespread use of consciousness technology. In this era of abundance the United States is able to invest more in foreign countries, and they too, under the tutelage of American psychic advisers, improve their productivity and economic base.

The increase in productivity has lessened inflation and made more money available for new investment. Interest rates have fallen as money becomes easily obtainable for loans. The first major effect is felt in the housing industry, as cheap loans spur construction of new housing.

INDUSTRY

Industrial corporations are among the first to make use of consciousness technology. Before tooling up for new, costly designs of major goods, they use psychic probes to find out how the public will react to their new designs. Using consciousness market research they obtain information about what the public will want, and then produce it. Better sales and fewer Edsel-type creations make for strong growth of industry.

Industrial engineers use consciousness technology to dream up highly efficient and cheaply produced innovations in many areas. By 1994 household robots are on the market. Hand-held computers are produced for school children and adults, who are learning sophisticated computer techniques for everyday application. Many industrial workers now work from home at their computer consoles, which are linked in to the main office.

By the year 2001 many corporations are using computerized automation in turning out new products. Former assembly-line workers now run machines, perform quality control, and use consciousness technology to refine manufacturing processes. Workers, with the aid of computer technology, become more efficient and need work only four days a week, many on their own schedules.

Companies now regularly send their management trainees to learn consciousness techniques at special academies. The trainees learn how to balance their brain functioning by using intuition and ESP along with logic to make the best decisions. Those who show the greatest intuitive talent climb the corporate ladder more quickly, and many become presidents of companies at an early age.

THE ARTS AND THE MEDIA

By 1990 the performing arts are beginning a renaissance that continues unabated into the year 2001. A significant by-product of the consciousness techniques taught in schools is the enhancement and development of artistic talent. Many young people discover talents they didn't know they had, even a significant number of adults are encouraged to dust off half-forgotten skills and talents. Everyone, it seems, has the need toward self-expression through music, dance, theater, art. Community groups spring up around the country as local showcases for the performing arts.

Amateur filmmaking becomes the rage as new technical processes make it possible for the average person to afford equipment to make three-reel movies. Writers, directors, actors, and other film contributors are found at community performing arts groups. Amateur film festivals become a popular pastime, as a new generation of film directors is born. People who used to show slides of their vacation trips now show their latest movies, some of which are good.

Hollywood movie studios, threatened by the competition, decide to finance certain talented amateur filmmakers to make professional-quality but low-budget movies that can be shown for less money than studio-produced films. Too many Hollywood blockbuster movies went bust, and tastes have changed; people look for creative, imaginative, and artistically produced products that inspire them to make their own movies better.

The explosion in amateur filmmaking spills over to television. Already beset by declining revenues because the public no longer wants the old formulas, the television industry looks for new products to match the new temper of the times. Now, instead of a malady-of-the-month movie, TV shows the most-creative-new-filmmaker movie of the month. More and more independent stations are taking away the markets of the major networks. These new stations are more innovative and offer opportunities for new filmmakers and others who show creative talent.

Television's soap operas are vanishing as daytime audiences discover it is more fun to make up and act in their own dramas than watching them on TV. Many former addicts of the soaps are now taking to writing their own episodes with their favorite characters and adding new characters from their own lives. Improvisational soap opera becomes a big hit at the community playhouses. Satires that combine several old soaps outdo Johnny Carson's *The Edge of Wetness;* one called *The Edge of Tomorrow* actually goes to Broadway.

Music is showing an astonishing diversity as new forms and instruments are combined with the human voice to achieve moving effects on listeners. The latest wave by 1991 is combining some of the rock 'n' roll sounds of the sixties with gospel-style lyrics to celebrate life in songs that inspire the audience to sing along. Sing-ins become a popular entertainment as more people become aware of the power of music to unite them in a single feeling and purpose. Some progressive churches begin to substitute this new wave for traditional hymns. The 1991 songs seem to sing themselves, expressing harmonically the richness of group feeling.

Pictorial art and sculpture take on a mystical quality by 1992. Using newly developed pigments that glow and shimmer, experimental artists create canvases of abstract yet strangely human forms, which have a joyous effect on the viewers. The newest form of art is light-painting, in which multicolored lasers are programmed by computer to make intricate, feathery designs in the night. Several banks and hotels now have nightly programs of light-painting that can be seen from the tops of their towers and delight viewers for miles around.

THE INDIVIDUAL

By the year 2001 the changes brought by consciousness technology are seen most dramatically in the individual. Having been trained to develop their intuitive and creative powers of mind, individuals become more spontaneous and given to pursuing the kind of life that they really want. As more opportunities become available, most people find that they do not have to work at a boring job; that both fulfillment and financial security are possible.

Young people no longer strive to dress and act alike, but delight in their individuality. They outdo each other in wearing distinctive, colorful clothes that reflect their personalities and moods. The advent of new fabrics makes individually styled clothes relatively cheap to make and encourages new designs. Both boys and girls learn how to design their own clothes.

Young people now grow up with a strong belief in themselves and their inner destiny. They are persistent in achieving their goals, which they realize can be fulfilled only in the context of society. They develop extraordinary skills at cooperating in mutual efforts.

Those who come to their early twenties in the year 2001 may be the most idealistic generation the world has known. But they are also practical, since they know that their inner destinies can be accomplished only by actually doing what they believe in. They take psychic abilities for granted. Anyone who tries to show off by bending spoons is laughed at as immature. The ideal role model for these young people is the person who effortlessly blends his or her psychic and logical powers of mind to accomplish new ideas and actions that benefit the community.

The heroes of 2001 are the brilliant achievers in the arts, business, science, technology, government, industry, medicine. The younger the achiever, the more he or she is admired.

The most prized quality for the geniuses of 2001 is *balance*—between logic and intuition, between individuality and group responsibility, between ego and service, between imagination and practicality, between dignity and a sense of humor, between receiving love and giving love.

The youth of 2001 take responsibility for their lives and their future. They know that they will create the best of what they can foresee. They believe in human destiny.

If these prophecies are fulfilled, it is we who can take the credit. If the flowers of the future bloom in a garden of Eden, it is we who will have planted them. Our generation is the guardian of destiny; we are the custodians of tomorrow.

The edge of tomorrow is *now*.

SOURCES

Note: The abbreviation *RIP* refers to *Research in Parapsychology*, the annual proceedings of the Parapsychological Association, published by Scarecrew Press, 52 Liberty St., PO Box 656, Metuchen, NJ 08840. Each year's proceedings are published the following year, and are edited variously by W. G. Roll, J. D. Morris, and R. L. Morris. *RIP* is the most complete source of current research in parapsychology.

The Parapsychological Association, founded in 1957, is the official scientific organization of parapsychology and is a member of the American Association for the Advancement of Science. Membership is restricted to active researchers and students, and numbers more than 260 members around the world. For information contact: The Parapsychological Association, PO Box 7503, Alexandria, VA 22307.

Chapter 1: Believing the Impossible
Page 15: Evaluation of the *National Enquirer* psychics appears in *The Book of Predictions*, by David Wallechinsky, Amy Wallace and Irving Wallace (NY: William Morrow, 1980), p. 403. Page 16: For my 1971 predictions see

Frank Foster, "Psychic Predicts Upsurge in Economy," *National Enquirer*, May 23, 1971. Page 16–17: Evaluation of my 1971 predictions is done by Henry Chase, "Cracks in the Crystal Ball," *Cheshire* (CT) *Herald*, December 27, 1973. Page 17–18: My 1981 predictions are reported by Paul Bannister, "Incredible Predictions of World's Most Successful Psychic," *National Enquirer*, November 4, 1980. Page 18: Predictions for 1975–1980 appear in *The People's Almanac*, by David Wallechinsky and Irving Wallace (Garden City, NY: Doubleday, 1975), pp. 1–30. Page 21: Fortune-tellers are analyzed by Emily P. Cary, "Telling on the Fortune-Tellers," *Psychic*, Vol. 7, No. 5 (1976), pp. 34–36. Page 28: The Iceland experiment was performed by Erlendur Haroldsson, "Reading Habits, Belief in ESP and Precognition," *RIP*, 1975, pp. 28–29.

Chapter 2: Premonitions
Page 33: David Booth's premonition is reported by Walter L. Lowe, "Bad Dreams in the Future Tense," *Playboy*, Vol. 27, No. 3 (1980), p. 102. Page 34: My assassination premonition is reported by Peter Fairley, "The Man Who Wrote 'I Fear Kennedy Assassination,' " London *Evening Standard*, June 7, 1968.

Chapter 3: Training Your Dream Tiger
Page 56: The Bessent precognitive dream studies appear in Chapter 14, "Dreaming of Things to Come," of *Dream Telepathy*, by Montague Ullman and Stanley Krippner with Alan Vaughan (New York: Macmillan, 1973). Page 59: *Living Your Dreams*, by Gayle Delaney (NY: Harper & Row, 1979).

Chapter 4: Experiments in Time
Page 73: Richard C. Neville's elevator-predicting experiment appears in "Some Aspects of Precognition Testing," *RIP*, 1975, pp. 26–31. Page 74: Helmut Schmidt's and J. B. Rhine's precognition experiments are summarized by

Douglas Dean, "Precognition and Retrocognition," in *Psychic Exploration*, by Edgar D. Mitchell and others, edited by John White (NY: Putnam's, 1974). Page 77: The SRI remote-viewing work is reported by Harold E. Puthoff and Russell Targ in "A Perceptual Channel for Information Transfer Over Kilometer Distances," *Proceedings of the IEEE*, Vol. 64 (1976), pp. 329–54, and is reprinted in *Mind at Large*, edited by C. Tart, H. Puthoff, and R. Targ (NY: Praeger, 1979). Page 77–78: The SRI experiment with Hella Hammid appears in H. E. Puthoff and Russell Targ, "Precognitive Remote Viewing," *RIP*, 1975, pp. 37–40. Page 79–80: Brenda Dunne and John Bisaha published their experiments in "Long Distance Precognitive Remote Viewing," *RIP*, 1975, pp. 68–70, and "Precognitive Remote Perception: A Critical Overview of the Experimental Program, "*RIP*, 1979, p. 117. Page 81–82: A final report by Gertrude Schmeidler and Michaeleen Maher appears in "Judges' Impressions of the Nonverbal Behavior of Psi-Conducive and Psi-Inhibitory Experimenters," *Journal of the American Society for Psychical Research*, July 1981. Page 87: The psychic prediction contest is taken from *The Book of Predictions*, by D. Wallechinsky and others (NY: William Morrow, 1980), p. 478, with permission of the authors.

Chapter 5: Making Contact
Page 91–92: My British election prediction is reported by Herb Kretzmer, "Mr. Big—Ready to Lead Britain, Says the Scholarly Prophet," London *Daily Express*, April 27, 1974. Page 96–97: The experiment with Carol Liaros is reported by Douglas Dean, "A Precognitive Method for Testing Sensitives," *RIP*, 1972, pp. 97–99. Page 107: The film *An Experiment with Croiset*, b & w, 29 min., is available for rental ($50) from Psycho-Physical Research Foundation, c/o Jule Eisenbud, M. D., 4634 E. 6th Ave., Denver, Colorado 80220. See also: Jule Eisenbud, "A Transatlantic Experiment in Precognition with Gerard Croiset," *Journal*

of the American Society for Psychical Research, Vol. 67, No. 16 (1973), pp. 1–25.

Chapter 6: Guiding Images

Page 113: Eleanor Friede is quoted by the editors of *Psychic*, in "Profiles in Business," *Psychic*, Vol. 6, No. 1 (1974), p. 30.

Chapter 7: The Art of Prophecy

Page 127: British journalist Peregrine Worsthorne speculates on Edward Kennedy in "The Fate of the Dynasty," London *Sunday Telegraph*, June 9, 1968. Page 133: The earthquake dream appears in my *Patterns of Prophecy* (NY: Hawthorn, 1973), pp. 182–83. Page 135: Barbara Honegger's report on the PA convention is entitled, "Quake Hits Parapsychology," *New Realities*, Vol. 3, No. 2 (1979), pp. 34–35. Page 138: *California Superquake, 1975–1977?* by Paul James (Hicksville, NY: Exposition Press, 1974). Page 139: *We Are the Earthquake Generation*, by Jeffrey Goodman (NY: Berkley Books, 1979). Page 139: *Pole Shift*, by John White (NY: Doubleday, 1980).

Chapter 8: The Science of Prediction

Page 146: The book *Executive ESP*, by Douglas Dean and John Mihalasky, is edited by Sheila Ostrander and Lynn Schroeder (Englewood Cliffs, NJ: Prentice Hall, 1974). Page 147: William Keeler is quoted by the editors of *Psychic*, "Profiles in Business," *Psychic*, Vol. 6, No. 1 (1974), p. 27. Page 149: *Profiles of the Future*, by Arthur C. Clarke (NY: Harper & Row, 1963). Page 150: Beverly Jaegers is quoted in *The Book of Predictions* on p. 284 and Alan Vaughan on p. 290. Page 153: Robert Silverberg is quoted by Michael Robertson, "There Is No Crystal Ball," *San Francisco Chronicle*, July 8, 1980. Page 157: The Mobius archaeological projects are reported by Stephan A. Schwartz, *The Alexandria Project* (NY: Delacorte-Friede, in press 1982).

Chapter 9: The Flexible Future
Page 161: Frances Vernier's premonition is reported under the title, "Woman's Amazing Psychic Dream Saves 39 from Fiery Death," *The Star*, April 7, 1981. Page 166: William G. Braud's formal report appears as "Project Chicken Little: A Precognition Experiment Involving the Skylab Space Station," *European Journal of Parapsychology*, Vol. 3, No. 2 (1980), pp. 149–65.

Chapter 10: Shaping Your Future
Page 176: The Santa Barbara studies are reported by Robert L. Morris, "The Airport Project: A Survey of the Techniques for Psychic Development Advocated by Popular Books," *RIP*, 1976, pp. 54–56; and by Robert L. Morris, Michael Nanko and David Phillips, "Intentional Observer Influence Upon Measurements of a Quantum Mechanical System," *RIP*, 1978, pp. 146–50. Page 176–77: The Yale study is reported by Ariel Levi, "The Influence of Imagery and Feedback on PK Systems," *RIP*, 1979, pp. 57–58. Page 177–78: The Simonton work is summarized by Judith Glassman, "They Beat Cancer," *Family Circle*, Vol. 94, No. 3 (February 24, 1981), p. 59. Page 186: The quote from Ben Bova is from his "The Role of Science Fiction," in *Science Fiction, Today and Tomorrow*, edited by Reginald Bretnor (Baltimore, MD: Penguin Books, 1975), p. 7, with permission of the author. Page 187: Roy Amara is quoted (in condensed form) from his "The Futures Field: Searching for Definitions and Boundaries," *The Futurist*, Vol. 15, No. 1 (1981), pp. 25–29.

Chapter 11: Time Will Tell
Page 198: Experimental tests of my theory are published in my report, "The Meaning of Coincidence," *Parapsychology Review*, Vol. 11, No. 4 (1980), pp. 9–12, available from the Parapsychology Foundation, 228 East 71st Street, New York, NY 10021.

RECOMMENDED READING

BARTLETT, Laile E. *Psi Trek: A World-Wide Investigation into the Lives of Psychic People and the Researchers Who Test Such Phenomena as: Healing, Prophecy, Dowsing, Ghosts, and Life After Death.* New York: McGraw-Hill, 1981. A good up-to-date popular introduction to the phenomena and researches of parapsychology.

CLARKE, Arthur C. *Profiles of the Future.* New York: Harper & Row, 1958; also paper. A classic study of technological predictions by science-fiction writers and scientists.

FISHER, Joe. *Predictions.* New York: Van Nostrand Reinhold, 1980. A popular excursion into past prediction of all types and some predictions for the future. Handsomely illustrated.

GREENHOUSE, Herbert. *Premonitions: A Leap into the Future.* New York: Bernard Geis, 1971; also paper. A fine compilation of premonitions, dream studies, and modern-day predictions by psychics.

MACKENZIE, Andrew. *The Riddle of the Future: A Modern Study of Precognition.* New York: Taplinger, 1975; also paper. A British study of precognitive phenomena that looks to quantum physics and consciousness studies for the answer.

VAUGHAN, Alan. *Incredible Coincidence: The Baffling World of Synchronicity.* New York: Lippincott, 1979; also paper. Precognitive phenomena are examined in the light of coincidence to produce a general theory about psychic phenomena.

VAUGHAN, Alan. *Patterns of Prophecy.* New York: Hawthorn, 1973; also paper. A critical study of prophetic experience that concludes that we have psychic blueprints of life. Contains predictions for the future.

WALLECHINSKY, David, Amy Wallace, and Irving Wallace. *The Book of Predictions.* New York: William Morrow, 1981. A massive compilation of predictions from all sources; stimulates future thought.